BR EMPIRE UNIFORMS 1919–1939

EDWARD HALLETT AND MICHAEL SKRILETZ

AMBERLEY

Acknowledgements

The authors wish to acknowledge the primary research of others that they have drawn upon to produce this work. Thanks go to many historians, predominantly Rog Dennis of Karkee Web for his work on accoutrements, Peter Suciu and Stuart Bates for their research into sun helmets, Martin Brayley for his advice and research into tropical uniforms and James Clowes for his support and assistance with identifying makers. Others, too numerous to mention, have contributed advice and information and we wish to thank them for their input. Our thanks go to Alan Hallett for proofreading the manuscript, Jeff and Lisa Skriletz for their help with photography and to our partners Emma Hallett and Anh Tran for supporting us on this project.

First published 2019

Amberley Publishing
The Hill, Stroud
Gloucestershire, GL5 4EP

www.amberley-books.com

British Library Cataloguing in Publication Data.
A catalogue record for this book is available from the British Library.

ISBN 978 1 4456 8894 7 (print)
ISBN 978 1 4456 8895 4 (ebook)

Typeset in 10pt on 12pt Sabon.
Typesetting and Origination by Amberley Publishing.
Printed in the UK.

Contents

1

Introduction

The period between 1919 and 1939 is often seen as a brief spell of peace between the terror of the two world wars and for the majority of the civilian population in both Great Britain and the Empire this was indeed the case. For the British Army and Navy, however, this period was a difficult one. On the one hand, colonial conflicts were still continuing much as they had in the late Victorian period, but on the other a central government in London was squeezing their resources to fight these wars in a way that had not been felt before. The interwar period was a time of disarmament and reduced military spending, both as the result of international treaties signed in the aftermath

Left: In the early 1930s, the Lewis gun was still in service as the Army's light machine gun. This air-cooled weapon used large drum magazines, each of which held forty-seven rounds of .303 ammunition. A number of pieces of equipment were devised to carry these magazines, their large circular shape being difficult to transport easily. Photographs of the Northamptonshire Regiment in 1932 show ammunition carriers in a Lewis gun section carrying two 'pouches, magazine, Lewis gun, web' on a standard pattern 1908 brace, slung around the neck over standard infantry equipment. This ammunition carrier is armed with the standard 'Rifle No. 1 Mk III*', to protect the Lewis gunner.

Right: This Lewis gun ammunition carrier has a 'matchet' attached to his belt. This was a 15-inch-long machete that was used for clearing vegetation to ensure the gun had a clear arc of fire. It was made of steel with a wood, leather or Bakelite handle and was carried in a leather scabbard on the belt.

of the First World War and in response to home-grown war-weariness. A major global depression in the period further squeezed funds and with huge surplus stockpiles of ships, armaments, uniforms and accoutrements left over from the First World War, there was little investment in either the Royal Navy or the Army. Only the RAF managed to receive new and relatively substantial funding in this period, its senior officers arguing persuasively to Parliament that they could control colonial incidents more effectively and cheaply from the air than the traditional method of putting boots on the ground.

The matchet was issued to NCOs and engineers on a regular basis. This example is dated 1917, but the pattern was to remain in service for decades to come. As a slashing tool, one edge is sharpened, while the tip is rounded and relatively blunt. It is carried in a leather scabbard with reinforcement fitted around the throat to prevent the blade from cutting and damaging the leather as it is drawn and replaced.

Webbing valises for carrying rifles were not particularly common, but examples were used in dusty conditions to help protect rifles from damage while not in use. This case was made by the Mills Equipment Company in 1936 and is shown with a Short Magazine Lee-Enfield rifle. This bolt-action rifle had a magazine that held ten rounds of .303 ammunition and was the service rifle across the British Empire throughout the interwar period.

Ammunition for Lee-Enfield rifles was issued in five-round charger clips. These were pieces of sprung metal that held the rounds securely until they were fed into the rifle. Although made obsolete in 1916, the Mk II charger (*left*) was still in service throughout the interwar period. Its replacement, the Mk IV (*right*), was designed to be less stiff and allowed the rounds to be fed into the rifle's magazine more easily. The loose Mk VII .303 round above the chargers was manufactured in 1931, the 'K' on the head stamp indicating it was produced by Kynoch.

Rifle slings were never patterned webbing items, but webbing slings were first approved for service in 1901. This example is stamped on one buckle to indicate that it was made by the Mills Equipment Company in 1936.

This lack of investment financially at the time in some ways foreshadowed a lack of intellectual investment in the period from military historians in the years since. There are relatively few books about the military in this period, and most are modest accounts of the campaigns fought by small groups of men. There has been no publication looking at what the men wore and carried in this period, many assuming it was just the same as for soldiers in either of the world wars. In reality, colonial warfare in the interwar period was very different from the large battles of either of the conflicts that bookend this period and one thing that is very apparent is the diversity of roles that the army, navy and air force had to perform. There was open warfare on the North West Frontier of India, the suppression of inter-religious rebellions in southern India, the protection of European mercantile interests in a fragmented Warlord China and the pursuit of pirates in the South China Seas. Meanwhile, away from combat, troops acted as policemen and peacekeepers for the League of Nations and performed a variety of ceremonial functions as representatives of the state across the four corners of the globe. This variety inevitably bled into what men wore and carried to perform these duties. Items of clothing and equipment from the First World War were modified and worn in new ways to meet the requirements of different theatres and new uniforms and accoutrements were designed and issued, albeit in small numbers, throughout the 1920s and early 1930s. The growing threat of war in Europe from a resurgent Germany in the mid-1930s led to a rapid modernisation of the equipment of the British Army and many of these new designs first saw service not in northern France, but in the far-flung corners of Empire where troops were stationed, fulfilling their usual peacetime roles in those last few years before war broke out once more.

New technology also influenced the equipment and uniforms worn between the wars. Aeroplanes and armoured cars took on an ever increasing importance in this period; these machines possessed as much psychological impact on indigenous populations as any practical utility. Both aeroplanes and armoured cars required careful mechanical handling in the hot sun of the colonies and both could be dirty and unreliable. This resulted in a need for specialist clothing that protected men from oil and dirt and specialist accoutrements to allow them to carry their weapons in the confines of a vehicle, surrounded by pieces of equipment that were easy to snag oneself upon. It was not only the crews of these aeroplanes and armoured cars who found their equipment altered by new machinery. The ordinary infantryman was now as likely to be transported by lorry as he was to march into base. This mechanisation was an active policy of the War Office throughout the interwar period and had an impact on load-bearing equipment. Men's personal loads became lighter and more focussed on essentials as equipment they had once had to carry could now be transported in a vehicle, ready when camp was made but safe and left to the rear when the men moved into action. The horse and the infantry's own footpower were never entirely replaced in this period, but both took on less significance in military planning as better roads and more reliable mechanised transport became available throughout the 1930s.

In an empire which covered a quarter of the world's landmass, it is unsurprising that the military might of the Crown differed very widely depending on which particular

Above left: This Royal Marine stands at ease waiting for an inspection to start in Malta in 1936. He wears the Royal Marines khaki drill tunic, which replaced the white cotton duck uniform in the early 1920s. This distinctive tunic features a mandarin-style standing collar, brass 'RM' titles on each epaulette, brass belt hooks and pointed cuffs. Each button has the anchor and laurel wreath badge of the Marines embossed onto it. He wears the Corps' whitened Wolseley helmet with large brass helmet plate on the front of it. For parade, he wears his pattern 1908 webbing in drill order, consisting of just the belt, bayonet and frog.

Above right: From the rear, it can be seen that this Marine has looped the two straps on the back of his pattern 1908 belt upwards and back through the two rear buckles. This was a method of smartening up the belt for parades and whenever the belt was to be worn on its own without shoulder braces.

The standard grenade in use by the British Army throughout the interwar period was the No. 36 Mk I 'Mills Bomb'. This grenade had been developed during the First World War and was the most successful of the early grenade designs, consisting of a cast-iron segmented body with a filling of Baratol explosive. These grenades were first shellacked to waterproof them in the First World War for service in Mesopotamia and this variant, known as the No. 36M Mk I, became the standard version in service across the Empire from 1932 into the 1970s. This example of the No. 36 was manufactured in 1918 and lacks the later waterproofing layer of shellac provided on the No. 36M grenade. The base plug of the grenade (*left*) was removable to allow the detonators to be inserted just before use. Carrying the grenades without detonators made them much safer to transport.

part of the world was in question. British regular troops were recruited in Great Britain and battalions were rotated out to various colonies, most often India, for a set period of time. These men were full-time professional soldiers and although the British Army was small compared to its European counterparts, it was entirely made up of volunteers and viewed itself as something of an elite force compared to the conscript armies of other countries. As well as these troops from Great Britain, local men were recruited across the Empire. In some places, such as India, these were native troops with British officers, their services supplemented by 'reliable' regiments from Great Britain. In other countries that were afforded more independence such as Canada, Australia and South Africa, forces were raised from local men as either professional full-time armies or as militias. As these countries were essentially self-governing, these troops were officered and commanded locally and there was no permanent British Army presence. Indeed, following the First World War even the foreign policy as regards to the deployment of these men was controlled at a local level rather than by London, hence the decision by the Canadian Government not to support Great Britain in military interventions during the Chanak Crisis in the 1920s.

This military autonomy extended to such things as purchasing uniforms and equipment and while the countries of the Empire tended to look to the mother country for guidance and inspiration on such matters, they were not required to follow the British Army's procurement decisions. This led to a number of interesting purchases by the governments of the Empire for their forces during the interwar period, with small

ARMY FORM B2557.

THE ARMY
THE FINEST JOB IN THE WORLD
WORK & PLAY ALL — OVER THE GLOBE
WHAT IT OFFERS AND HOW TO JOIN

Recruitment pamphlets were produced during the interwar period to encourage men to sign up for the army. Some were drawn by the prospect of regular food and money in their pockets, especially from the areas of Britain worst hit by the global depression. The army emphasised the opportunities to play sports and see the world, however, feeling that this would best appeal to the right sort of young man.

batches of non-standard equipment that were often more up-to-date in design than those used in Great Britain. While most of the equipment ordered for the armies of the Empire came from Great Britain, there was also a move in the period between the wars to set up production in the various individual countries. These early developments in local military production were cautious at best, but they were to sow the seeds for the far greater diversification of production in the Second World War. The individual governments of the Empire were keen to develop their own local industries not only for domestic reasons, such as encouraging employment in depressed parts of their states, but also to help move away from the reliance on Great Britain and the resultant higher cost of importation of items that could potentially be manufactured locally.

Left: This naval rating from the late 1930s stands ready for exercise, carrying his General Service Respirator in a Mark VA haversack. This is worn in the typical arrangement for naval personnel, with the shoulder strap lengthened and worn across the body and a waist strap fitted to hold the haversack in position. The rating wears the second pattern of naval sun helmet, introduced in 1936.

Right: This sailor carries the standard issue Admiralty 301 pattern clasp knife on a lanyard around his waist. The knife featured both a blade and a large marlin spike for working with lines, an essential task for all sailors. This sailor is not wearing the traditional jean collar in this working rig, but the large flap of fabric on the rear of his jumper is visible along with his name, which has been inked onto the reverse.

In 1936, the Royal Navy introduced a new pattern of sun helmet. This differed from the earlier pattern in having a much squarer profile to the rear of the helmet, much more similar to that used in the Wolseley pattern. This offered greater protection to the wearer's neck than the earlier model. The design was slowly phased in through the final years before the Second World War and would be the last sun helmet adopted by the Royal Navy before the use of such helmets in the tropics was abandoned completely.

The Mk V respirator haversack replaced the old small box respirator haversack used in the First World War. It had a separate internal pocket to carry anti-gas ointment and anti-gas eye-shields, although this was never large enough for everything a man might be issued. The most important improvement was the shoulder strap, which could be detached at one end by means of a brass spring clip attaching to a brass D-ring on the haversack. This allowed the haversack to be reconfigured for different methods of carriage without needing to be taken to a regimental tailor. For normal marching order the strap was attached to the D-ring and adjusted to rest on the left hip or moved to the chest in 'alert' position. The RAF and Royal Navy used long hose respirators, with the haversack worn at the waist so it did not interfere with equipment a man was operating. In this configuration the haversack was issued with a waist strap and re-designated the Mk Va (*middle*). In the cavalry configuration (*bottom*), the shoulder strap was attached to the left lower D-ring of the haversack, which ensured the haversack sat at the right angle on the cavalryman's upper back. The cord loop on the shoulder strap was secured over one of the man's shirt buttons to prevent it from sliding around the body.

This Royal Navy Mk IV service respirator is an early example with all components dated 1928 or 1929 except the Type E Mk IV filter, which is dated 1938 and painted tan. The respirator is a long hose example that allowed the filter canister to be worn at the waist. The tab on the hose has an eyelet that could be connected to a brass hook on the haversack strap, thus supporting the weight of the hose and preventing it from pulling the face piece down and compromising the gasproof seal.

The subject of the British Empire and colonial military operations remains controversial in some quarters to this day. This book does not seek to pass judgement on the men and decisions made eighty or ninety years ago, but rather to study the uniforms and equipment of the ordinary soldiers and officers who served the King around the globe and offer some examples of the typical operations Empire troops found themselves undertaking in the interwar period. The reconstructions in this book are based on period photographs and the authors have made every effort to make these as accurate as possible. Some of these reconstructions feature unique and unusual pieces of uniform and equipment, the pictures of which have not been published before; others depict more familiar items but worn in a way and combination that is typical of the military serving in the Empire in this period. These reconstructions are accompanied by detailed photographs of various artefacts from the authors' collections that illustrate some of the developments in military equipment in this period. Due to the scarcity of some items of native uniform today, those troops that wore the more exotic items of uniform are represented by period cigarette cards that allow these men to be represented in a way that would not be possible through modern reconstructions. The study of British Empire troops in this period has been long overlooked and the authors hope that this book goes some way to redressing this oversight, while also acting as a useful introduction to the period for the reader.

The khaki drill officer's uniform was based closely on the barathea service dress worn on Home Service, with an open collar worn with shirt and tie. The jacket has pleated patch pockets on each breast and large bellowed pockets on the skirts, secured with removable brass regimental buttons. Rank is worn on the shoulder straps and the insignia, like the buttons, would be made of brass and removable to protect the uniform during the washing needed in tropical stations. It is worn with a cloth belt, although this could be substituted for a leather Sam Browne belt for more formal occasions. The trousers are cut in the style of riding breeches, as even officers in infantry regiments rode horses much of the time. This officer wears brown boots and cloth puttees and has a privately purchased Wolseley helmet on his head, which is edged in leather to help protect the rim.

2

China, Hong Kong and the Far East

The British Empire stretched across the globe and at one stage a quarter of the world's landmass was ruled by the Crown in London. British possessions in the Far East were a tiny proportion of this in terms of the number of square miles they covered, but in terms of Britain's position as the predominant global trading nation they were essential strategically. The various ports and enclaves in China were especially crucial in keeping the trade routes of the region open, with the ports being used not only for direct trade regionally and globally, but also as essential refuelling stations for the Royal Navy. In this maritime environment it is unsurprising that the Royal Navy came to prominence in a way the army did not and arguably this power reached its zenith in the period between the wars.

It is 1938 and this private soldier in Singapore has been issued a set of the new 'web equipment, pattern 1937', introduced into service a few months before. He still carries the venerable Short Magazine Lee-Enfield rifle. He wears 'Bombay Bloomers', khaki drill shorts that featured large turn-ups that were designed to be undone, thus increasing the length of the shorts and protecting the lower legs from the cooler evening temperatures of the tropics and the risk of mosquito bites. Here the shirt is a collarless aertex example, produced in India with bone buttons. This private wears the Mk I steel helmet that had been in service since the First World War. A new, updated version was still in the process of being introduced when war broke out in 1939.

A view from the side shows the larger size of the new pattern 1937 haversack, far deeper than that issued with the pattern 1908 webbing. This was designed to carry both mess tins and water bottle, but soldiers moved the bottle to the right hip to free up more space in the haversack. The scabbard for his bayonet is fitted with a khaki drill cover, a common practice in tropical areas, probably to help protect his uniform from marks that might arise from the waxed black leather scabbard.

Early in the interwar period, the pattern 1908 webbing was identical to that used during the First World War. The entrenching tool and helve carrier were still worn, along with the earlier pattern of water bottle carrier with the front-securing press stud. These features were slowly changed as the 1920s progressed and time became available to reflect on what designs best suited a peacetime army. Note the blue enamelled Mk VI water bottle in its thick, khaki felt cover. The cork stopper is tied to an 18-inch stopper cord, which is sewn directly onto the felt cover.

Above left: The Legation District was a section of Peking established after the Second Opium War which contained international legations, or embassies. This part of the city was not under Chinese law and was run by the various powers which had legations there. It was surrounded by a high wall with a total area of just 4,300 feet by 2,300 feet. In the wake of the Boxer Rebellion, the various powers were allowed a military presence here and the British garrisoned around a hundred men. This private has arrived in the legation and waits to be allocated his bunk in the barracks. He is wearing woollen service dress with a sun helmet, typical dress in the cooler northern regions of China. The service dress had been introduced in 1902 and had undergone minor changes a number of times before the end of the First World War. The uniform was recut in 1922 to make it more tailored, thus giving it a smarter appearance and making it more suitable as a parade uniform. As this private has been travelling, the action of his rifle is protected from dust with a canvas cover and he carries a large canvas kitbag with his extra uniforms and personal kit.

Above right: This soldier wears the full pattern 1908 set in Marching Order. In this configuration, the haversack is moved to below the waist and a large pack is carried on the back. A pair of supporting straps cross the pack and attach to straps coming from the rear of the ammunition pouches; these help balance out the weight of the pack and make it more comfortable to wear for long periods.

To help prevent theft from kit bags, brass locks were provided. The straight bar was threaded through the eyelets at the neck of the kitbag; the curved section was then closed and a padlock could be fitted to the hole to prevent the lock being removed. The curved section then doubled as a carrying handle. This example was made in India but the design is identical to that used across the Empire. To discourage theft from kitbags, men were issued with small brass padlocks that could be used to secure the kit bag lock. This padlock was manufactured by Walsall Locks & Cart Gear Ltd in 1925 and is marked with the War Department Broad Arrow.

Shanghai

The British had a presence in Shanghai, China, as early as 1842 following the Chinese defeat in the First Opium War. Five ports were opened to foreign trade, ending a monopoly on trade through the port of Canton. While Hong Kong had full British sovereignty, Shanghai was still technically under Chinese rule, but an international settlement was quickly established and in effect the city was run by the British with some assistance from other foreign nationals in the city.

By the 1920s the rest of China had descended into civil war with numerous warlords fighting each other for control of territory and resources in the aftermath of the fall of the Qing dynasty in 1912. For the most part this did not affect the British in their enclave of Shanghai, as they controlled the city and the European powers garrisoned well-equipped troops in the city to protect it alongside a local militia called the Shanghai Defence Force. In January 1927, however, the British authorities became concerned by the advance of the Chinese National Revolutionary Army under Chiang Kai Shek, which was advancing towards the city. To protect their interests, the British Army dispatched a force of sixteen Rolls-Royce armoured cars and a company of the Royal Tank Regiment to the city to bolster the garrison. These men patrolled the city alongside their French and US Marine Corps counterparts and the armoured cars discouraged most forms of violence against the European powers.

Period photographs of British troops in Shanghai in 1927 show them wearing a very relaxed form of tropical dress. Due to the heat, just shorts and collarless shirts were worn with socks, puttees and a Wolseley helmet to protect their heads from the sun. This simple uniform gave the troops maximum mobility, unencumbered by tight parade tunics, and was paired with the most basic of equipment, with most men wearing just a 1908 pattern haversack slung over the shoulder as a satchel with a shoulder brace as the strap. Over this was worn a 1908 pattern belt and bayonet frog with spare rounds of ammunition presumably carried in either the soldier's haversack or pockets.

This private in Shanghai, 1927, stands next to a Rolls-Royce armoured car waiting to patrol the streets of the city and protect the interests of the many Western citizens of the International Settlement. He is simply dressed for maximum mobility, wearing a pair of khaki drill shorts and a grey collarless woollen shirt. He wears a Wolseley helmet and is armed with an SMLE rifle, the sling lengthened in preparation for operations. His webbing is a curious setup with a pattern 1908 haversack worn as a shoulder bag, using a shoulder brace as a cross strap. His 1908 belt, on which his sword bayonet is carried in its frog, is worn over the strap of the haversack, keeping it pressed to the side of his waist and preventing it from bouncing around when he runs. This modification appears to have been a local adaptation and is seen in several photographs of the incident. Though many men seem to have adopted this interesting configuration, it does not appear later in other skirmishes.

The situation around Shanghai remained tense for a couple of years, but by 1929 the threat was deemed to have subsided to such a degree that the armoured cars could be withdrawn and the security of the city left to the police, militia and standard infantry garrison. Britain would maintain a presence in Shanghai until 1940, when all British troops were withdrawn as the threat from the Japanese in the region became ever greater and the risk of garrisoning the city was deemed too great for any benefits that might have come about from the city remaining in British possession.

Yangtze River

A few months before the deployment of the armoured cars to Shanghai, tensions had boiled over into an armed skirmish on the Yangtze River at the treaty port of Wanhsien. Rivers were the easiest way for local warlords to move their troops around China and, lacking their own ships, warlords frequently commandeered foreign cargo vessels for the purpose. Although international merchant ships agreed not to offer their services to these warlords, only the British and Americans had sufficiently powerful gunboats on the river to enforce this neutrality. In August 1926 a warlord named Yang Sen arrived at the treaty port of Wanhsien and tried to extort money from the foreign cargo

HMS *Gannet* was a river gunboat built specifically for service on the Yangtze River. She was built in Yarrow in Great Britain in 1927 and she spent the interwar years patrolling the river. She was armed with two 3-inch guns and eight machine guns. The typical crew included two officers, six petty officers and leading seamen with seventeen able seamen. The rest of the fifty or so crew were locally recruited men who took on roles such as cooks, deckhands and stokers.

vessels in the port for a spurious 'wharfage tax'. The British vessels, which included two British vessels of the China Navigation Company, refused to pay these charges and on 26 August a small party of Yang's men boarded the SS *Wanhsien* and tried to commandeer it to move troops. A party of armed sailors from the gunboat HMS *Cockchafer* was dispatched and managed to persuade Yang's men to leave. Having failed to appropriate the SS *Wanhsien*, Yang's men then turned to another ship from the same company, the SS *Wanliu*, and attempted to board her. The captain of the SS *Wanliu* steamed off as fast as the ship could manage to avoid capture and, in the process, swamped and sank a couple of local sampans.

This gave Yang a pretext for taking action and after negotiations had broken down his men seized both the SS *Wanhsien* and another ship, the SS *Wantung*, and took their crews prisoner. With 20,000 enemy troops in the port of Wanhsien with shore-based artillery, the two local Royal Navy gunboats were outgunned and had to hold back from action. The local Royal Navy commander decided that a rescue of the British crews was essential, and ideally it would be best to recapture the two vessels in the hands of Yang's men.

In order to accomplish these objectives, he commandeered the SS *Kia Wo* and armed the vessel with a 2-pounder pom-pom and machine guns, adding armour plates and sandbags to give it some protection. A scratch naval boarding party was pulled together from men of the cruiser HMS *Despatch* and the two gunboats *Mantis* and *Scarab* and the ship sailed into the port of Wanhsien, trying to appear as much like a merchant ship, rather than a naval vessel, as possible. The subterfuge did not last

Above left: The Royal Navy maintained a constant presence on the Yangtze River during the interwar period and this lieutenant is serving aboard HMS *Cockchafer* in 1926. This kidney-shaped bag was in use by the Royal Navy throughout the 1920s, and would have originally contained a Mk III respirator or, by the late 1920s, a Mk IV respirator. This officer wears the standard white cotton service uniform worn by all officers in tropical climates. Removable rank straps attach to each shoulder with cords, allowing them to be removed when the uniform needed to be laundered. His web equipment is the Royal Navy's pattern 1919 set, with the holster designed for the large .455 Mk VI revolver that was common issue during the period. The cutlass remained in service right up until the Second World War, offering a silent and effective weapon when boarding an enemy ship. Here the lieutenant carries an 1889 pattern which featured a cast-iron ribbed grip, basket hilt and double-edged spear point tip. His binoculars are naval issue with prominent yellow painted Broad Arrow marks on the top.

Above right: The leather scabbard for the cutlass hangs down below the belt and its long length is visible, a hazard when manoeuvring in the close confines of a ship. The 'bottle, water, Mk VI' is visible in the pattern 1919 carrier. This carrier used thinner 1-inch straps than the earlier pattern 1908 design, but continued to have a long top strap with front closure stud. This feature was modified on pattern 1908 carriers from 1921 onwards and was not found on Mills' webbing designs after this date, but 1919 carriers continued to have the front closure until the pattern ceased production around 1940.

Above left: The Royal Navy used a unique kidney-shaped haversack for its respirators in the interwar period. This haversack was slung across the body and held steady with a waist strap secured by a large plain brass buckle. Press studs were fitted at one end of the haversack to give access to the respirator and hooks were fitted to the shoulder strap to help support the weight of the hose. This haversack was used with both the Mk II respirator and the later Mk IV respirator before the Royal Navy adopted the Mk V haversack in the 1930s.

Above right: The .455 service revolver remained the most common sidearm for British officers and those not armed with a rifle in the interwar period. Webley had been the main manufacturer of these revolvers since the 1880s; however, this example was produced by the Royal Small Arms Factory, Enfield, in 1925 as stamped on the frame (*inset*). The design breaks at the top, with an automatic extractor built into the cylinder that ejected all six spent cases in one movement. Officers continued to purchase their own revolvers, and were permitted to choose which manufacturer they wanted, as long as the ammunition was easily available through military channels.

long and as Yang's forces opened fire on the vessel, her red ensign was dropped and the navy's white ensign run up the mast. Fierce fighting then ensued, with the men on the SS *Kia Wo* boarding the SS *Wanhsien* and freeing her crew, who were quickly transferred to the rescue ship. While this was going on, HMS *Cockchafer* bombarded key points in the treaty port to prevent Yang's men from co-ordinating a counter attack. When the SS *Kia Wo* retreated, however, it could not be said that the action had been an unqualified success. Although the crews of the merchant ships had been rescued, a greater number of the boarding party had been killed than the number of those saved from captivity and both merchantmen remained in the hands of the warlord.

Royal Navy ratings serving on China's navigable rivers were dressed in the white tropical uniform worn by all seaman ratings in tropical climes. This was paired with the Royal Navy sun helmet, a white pith helmet that included beckets to allow a cap tally to be worn. Sailors armed with rifles would also be equipped with standard 1908 pattern webbing, often marked with an 'N' in ink or stamped into the brass to indicate naval ownership. Most ships were equipped with an armoury of rifles, pistols and cutlasses to be issued to men for landing and boarding parties, along with a supply of webbing equipment that could be handed out to the men to accompany their weapons. It was from these stores that the men who took part in the rescue mission would have drawn their weapons and equipment prior to setting out on the raid, though steel helmets replaced the sun helmet during the operation and jumpers were not worn.

Above left: This rating from the cruiser HMS *Despatch* stands waiting to go aboard the SS *Kia Wo* before it steams into Wanhsien to rescue the crews of two merchant ships that were being held captive by the warlord Yang Sen. The rating wears the white cotton duck uniform used by the Royal Navy in the tropics and the Royal Navy issue sun helmet. He wears pattern 1908 webbing over his uniform and high Mills Pattern Naval Leggings over his boots. He will likely discard his jumper and replace his sun helmet with a steel helmet for the coming action.

Above right: From the rear, it can be seen that this sailor has followed the photos, rather than the fitting instructions, of the 1920 *Royal Naval Handbook of Field Training* and has attached his water bottle to the haversack, which is worn high on his back. The pattern 1908 webbing set still retains the entrenching tool and cover, despite this component having been dropped by the Army. The Royal Navy continued to issue it and ordered new examples of the cover until the 1908 pattern was displaced in the Second World War. The accompanying helve for the entrenching tool can be seen hanging down on the opposite side, next to the bayonet scabbard.

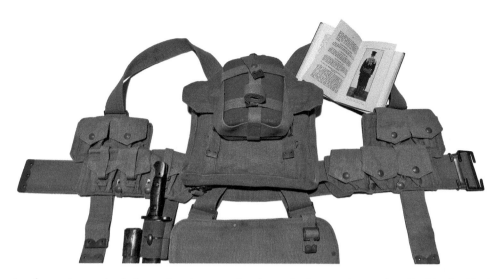

An alternative method of carrying the water bottle on the haversack was described in the 1934 *Royal Naval Handbook of Field Training*, which called for the tabs on the haversack to be passed through the buckles on the water bottle carrier with a supporting strap used to secure the bottle. This was passed round the bottle and after being secured through the buckle, the end was rolled back to give a smart military appearance. This method kept the water bottle from bouncing around while the sailor moved.

Sun helmets for ratings were introduced by the Royal Navy in 1921 to replace straw sennet hats in tropical regions. Made of cork, these helmets had a six-panel construction with a wide, flat oval brim. The tradition of wearing cap ribbons on sennet hats was continued on this pattern of helmet and cloth loops were added to the band to hold the ribbon in place. This example was made by Everitt W. Vero & Co. in London in 1936 and is fitted with an HMS *Despatch* cap ribbon.

Hong Kong

The Far East was very much the domain of the Royal Navy and between the wars the Royal Navy China Station was based predominantly at Hong Kong, with the fleet normally consisting of a cruiser squadron, a flotilla of twelve submarines, the Yangtze flotilla of ten gunboats and the West River flotilla with a further five of these small craft. The station also boasted a flotilla of nine destroyers and a single aircraft carrier, usually the HMS *Hermes*. Although the altercations with local warlords were some of the most spectacular skirmishes in the region, most day-to-day work for the navy consisted of hunting down the pirates who preyed on the merchant ships of the region. The Australian newspaper *The Newcastle Sun* reported one of these punitive expeditions in its edition of 25 March 1927.

It is hoped that piracy on the waters between Hong Kong and Canton has been checked by the destruction of pirate villages by a British naval force.

A message from Hong Kong states that a British naval expedition against the notorious Chinese pirates' lair in Bias Bay made a thrilling story of adventure.

The expedition, which was commanded by Rear-Admiral Boyle, and comprised the cruisers *Frobisher* and *Delhi*, the mine-sweeper *Marazion*, the sloop *Foxglove*, and the aircraft carrier *Hermes*, left Hong Kong on Tuesday evening and arrived off Bias Bay early the following morning.

Three hundred naval men and police embarked in boats, which the *Marazion* towed ten miles to the head of the Inlet, where the men waded ashore in waist-deep muddy water, and found the two villages which were the pirate haunts, deserted. The inhabitants were hiding in trees.

The villagers were collected and given a period of grace to collect their belongings, after which houses, sheds, junks and sampans were destroyed. Meanwhile aeroplanes from the *Hermes* flew over the scene. The neighbouring hillocks were crowded around with Chinese people watching the operations. The smoke of the burning mat sheds was visible for miles around, making a salutary object lesson in the district.

The operations were attended without casualties to either side. Instructions not to injure buildings of a religious character were carefully observed.

Copies of explanatory notices regarding the object of the punitive expedition; with a warning against a recurrence of piracies were distributed in the villages.

Men boarding suspected pirate junks or landing at notorious pirate bases such as Bias Bay went heavily armed, carrying pistols and cutlasses as a handier alternative to a

Ammunition was supplied in wooden boxes, this example being the H3 Mk I box for .303 rifle rounds. The box is strongly made with a wire handle to allow it to withstand the rigours of transport. The lid is wedge-shaped and secured with a removable brass pin. These boxes had an internal sealed tin lining to further protect the ammunition. The contents are indicated by a paper label pasted to one side which indicates that this box holds 360 rounds of Mk VII ammunition packed in cases.

Royal Navy shooting competition between crews from the heavy cruiser HMS *Hawkins*, light cruiser HMS *Despatch* and sloop HMS *Bluebell* in China around 1923. Note the use of cap ribbons on the ratings' sun helmets, while the petty officers have puggarees on their helmets. The Royal Marine, in khaki drill, has a white Wolseley helmet fitted with a helmet plate. A Wolseley pattern helmet can also be seen on the officer in the back, with its blue stripe at the top fold of the puggaree. H3 ammunition boxes loaded with .303 inch Mk VII ammunition litter the ground.

The Admiralty 301 pattern clasp knife was introduced in about 1910 and had a folding blade and marlinspike with a staghorn handle. A copper shackle allowed the clasp knife to be secured to a lanyard. It was officially replaced by a new pattern in 1929 but continued to see service for many years.

rifle on-board the cramped passageways of a ship or the back streets of a pirate village. In these conditions range was less important and handy short-range weapons, such as revolvers and bladed weapons, were more than adequate when the distance could be measured in single yards.

With so much reliance on pistol and cutlass, the Navy looked for a new webbing set to replace the 1908 pattern, which was fine for rifle-equipped troops but poorly adapted for holsters and pistol ammunition. The resultant set was supplied by the Mills Equipment Company and came to be known as the 1919 pattern set. It had thinner and lighter belts and shoulder braces, a wedge-shaped haversack and a large rucksack with provision for strapping a blanket or an oilskin around the outside. This pattern was very much adapted for naval use as it offered greater carrying capacity compared with earlier models, an important consideration when a landing party might be out of contact with their ship for several days and needed to carry everything on their own backs. The holster with this set was designed to carry the .455 Webley revolver and featured a wooden plug in the base to protect the muzzle of the weapon. A large pouch was worn on the belt to carry extra ammunition and a special frog to carry the cutlass was also provided. Naval ownership was again indicated by both ink 'N' stamps and the pressing of this initial into the brass fittings of the various components.

The pattern 1919 web equipment set was designed by the Mills Equipment Company as a replacement for the British Army's pattern 1908 set. The design was constructed around a three-piece waist belt with an adjustable back strap. The Army was not interested, however, as there were millions of sets of pattern 1908 equipment in store after the First World War, and so Mills adapted its new design for use with cutlass and pistol and sold it to the Royal Navy. A wedge-shaped haversack could be carried either on the back or below the waist, as seen here, and a large rucksack was provided. A frog for a cutlass could also be provided and was similar in design to the pattern 1908 bayonet frog, but with different dimensions. The Navy did not place huge orders, but production continued from the early 1920s through to about 1940 when the design was replaced with the pattern 1937 set.

The pattern 1919 rucksack was designed with a strap on the top flap to secure a mess tin carrier. Older designs of carrier required the strap to be unbuckled before the mess tin could be accessed, so a new webbing mess tin carrier design was developed in the early 1920s that made it possible to remove the mess tins for use, even with the carrier attached to the rucksack.

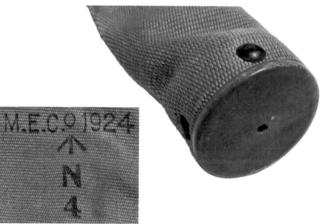

Many items of web equipment produced for the Navy were marked with both a Broad Arrow and an 'N', stamped into the brass fittings to indicate RN ownership (*left*). Pattern 1919 webbing was also ink-stamped with a naval acceptance mark, such as these markings on a 1924-dated pistol case (*middle*). The first pattern of 1919 pistol case had a wooden plug at the tip to protect the muzzle of the holstered revolver (*right*).

The ports of Hong Kong and Wei Hei Wei were postings much sought after by soldiers and sailors in the interwar period. They offered exotic surroundings with numerous opportunities for relaxation and excellent facilities for the European visitor. With prestigious clubs for officers and men, such as the Royal Hong Kong Yachting Club and the China Fleet Club, Hong Kong especially was regarded as a jewel in the crown of Empire in the Far East. Despite this fact, clouds were on the horizon and in 1927 the garrison was increased, firstly in response to the violence in the rest of China during the Warlord era and then in the face of growing Japanese aggression in the region. This way of life would come abruptly to an end with the Japanese invasion of 1941.

3

India between the Wars

If the Far East largely fell under the influence of the Royal Navy, India was the purview of the Army. India was not, however, garrisoned by a single homogenous army between the wars, but rather three separate types of military forces were to be found in the subcontinent. Firstly, there was the British Army made up of British troops and regiments sent out from the United Kingdom for a fixed period of time to serve in India. There was also the Indian Army, which had British officers and Indian other ranks and was recruited and paid for by the Indian Government. Finally, India also had a number of state armies. Under the British Raj, a number of Indian princes retained local powers and rights to rule sections of India with permission from the Indian Government and many of the more prosperous princes maintained their own personal armies. The quality of the soldiers in India varied, with British and Indian Army units

Bikanir State was one of the princely states of Imperial India and maintained a small state army. In 1935, the state's military consisted of a battery of artillery, two motor machine-gun sections, two squadrons of lancers and an infantry battalion. This captain is from the Ganga Risala, a mounted camel corps, and he wears the full dress uniform. Unlike the brightly coloured dress uniforms seen in other regiments, this regiment based its dress uniform on the khaki drill field uniform. Dress additions to this uniform include red-faced and heavily embroidered cuffs, a red and gold cummerbund around the waist and an elaborate turban. None of these features would be suitable in the field, but illustrate how the traditional combat uniform evolved into parade dress in some regiments.

being well trained and usually fairly well equipped. The armies of the Indian princes were more variable in quality, with some being little more than ceremonial bodyguards and others better trained and equipped along British lines. By the late 1930s, some of these state armies could boast machine-gun companies and mechanised infantry units as local princes and maharajas invested in their militaries as symbols of personal power and bargaining tools with the British, who might ask for their services in any upcoming conflict.

Despite there being three different types of military forces in India, there would never have been enough troops to garrison the whole subcontinent fully and the army was instead used to aid the civilian power rather than as an occupying force. There were a number of military towns, called cantonments, across the country and these were used to garrison and train troops. These cantonments were situated in areas that the British felt were healthy, i.e. places that had a more temperate climate and less danger from tropical diseases. Around the cantonment, towns quickly sprang up with merchants, tinkers, servants and prostitutes to service the army. A couple of times a year, military units would march from one cantonment to another. This decampment helped move troops to more comfortable billets as the weather changed, provided much-needed relief from the frequent boredom of garrison life, and 'showed the flag' as the massed men of a regiment marched through the countryside in a display of military might.

Typically, men marched short distances and were moved by rail for longer journeys, but throughout the interwar period the roads of India were improved and mechanised transport became ever more important to the army. Indeed, the need of the army was the biggest factor in the improvement of internal communications within India and most of the earliest metalled roads were between military settlements. Although these roads were not necessarily built for the encouragement of local and regional trade, all benefitted from the improved communications that the roads brought.

As in other parts of the Empire with similar climates, the most common uniforms worn in India were khaki drill, with the tropical version of the service dress in use throughout this period. This mirrored its woollen counterpart and had a rise and fall collar, secured with brass hooks and eyes, and was fastened up the front by a series of removable buttons, either with the regiment's crest on it or, more typically, the General Service Royal coat of arms. This tunic was paired with a pair of trousers that was

The 17-inch pattern 1907 sword bayonet was re-designated the 'Bayonet No. 1 Mk I' in 1926. During the interwar period, most bayonets in use were left over from the First World War, though some limited production occurred, such as this 1921 example made by the Rifle Factory Ishapore in India. The inset shows a close-up of the markings on the ricasso.

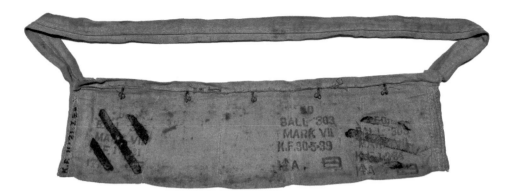

.303 rifle ammunition was frequently supplied pre-packaged in cotton bandoliers. Each bandolier had five pockets secured with brass hooks, which could hold two five-round chargers, giving a total of fifty rounds. These bandoliers could be slung over the body to provide easily accessible ammunition in a firefight. Although technically disposable, they were often collected up, refilled and reissued. This example was manufactured in India in 1921 and reissued four times with the old stampings cancelled and new ones applied.

identical in cut and style to the woollen service dress. Until the mid-1930s, this uniform was worn for both ceremonial and operational purposes. In the mid-1930s, khaki drill shorts and tropical shirts became universally issued and the traditional service dress was reserved for ceremonial wear.

The standard of dress required of British troops on parade in India reached new heights between the wars with one soldier remarking, 'a speck you got away with on parade at Aldershot was like an ink stain on the parade ground at Poona'. Another private soldier recalled, 'the turn out of the battalion when I first saw it dazzled me. I had never seen such smart soldiers whose uniforms were washed and ironed every day.' These high standards, however, were easier to meet due to the low cost of local labour. Even a private soldier could afford a few annas to have a native servant clean and press his uniform, polish his boots and brasso his belt buckle, with a hot shave from a native barber, called a 'nappy wallah', a daily ritual for most.

Officers also mirrored their service dress in the lighter khaki drill uniform, retaining their regimental distinctions and idiosyncrasies, but in a lighter fabric. Shirts and ties continued to be worn, even on campaign, as a symbol of the officer's status. For the evenings, when temperatures were a little cooler, mess dress was worn by officers just as it was in Britain. Officers often had local tailors, such as the famous firm of Ranken & Co. of 'Calcutta, Simla, Lahore and Rawal Pindi', make up mess dress in their regimental colours, but of a slightly lighter weight wool than was typical in cooler climes. Despite being able to choose a more comfortable fabric, mess dress continued to be worn with starched shirts and black tie, regardless of the climate.

Native regiments also typically wore khaki drill, but cut in a traditional Indian style. The most common garment was a collarless shirt, called a kurta, that fitted over the head and came down to the knee. Kurtas used by the Indian Army typically had two pleated pockets on the breast and a pair of shoulder straps to display the

Above left: This private from the East Yorkshire Regiment is depicted in parade dress in India in the 1930s. For parades a simplified version of the pattern 1903 leather bandolier equipment was often used. This was known as Drill Order and consisted of a leather waist belt, two Mk II leather fifteen-round ammunition pouches and a bayonet frog. This provided a smart order of equipment and was light enough that it did not cause excessive fatigue if a man was standing in the heat of the Indian sun for prolonged periods. His Wolseley helmet has a cherry red felt puggaree flash bearing an embroidered 'XV', the old regimental number of the East Yorkshire Regiment. The cap badge is worn on the front and centre of his sun helmet.

Above right: For parades it was common for soldiers to be issued sword bayonets that had been chromed. The wearing of puttees was not always observed for parade use, and here the soldier wears the cuffs of his trousers loose so they fall over his boots and rest a short distance from the ground. As he is on parade, the sling of the rifle is tightened so that it is taut against the underside of the rifle and presents a soldierly appearance.

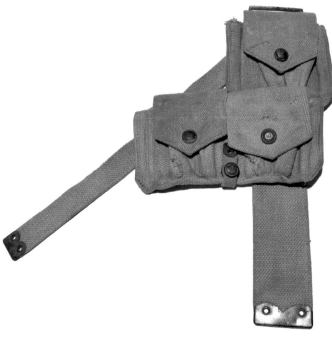

The standard pattern 1908 cartridge carrier held seventy-five rounds in five pockets. A variation was produced for India which only had three pockets, for a total of forty-five rounds. Little is known about these carriers, but it seems they were intended for soldiers of smaller stature who could not comfortably wear the five-pocket version. This example was made by Michael Wright & Son Ltd in 1938 and bears an Indian Broad Arrow acceptance mark.

Above left: Canvas water buckets with rope handles were in common use by military units to fetch water for washing, cleaning and watering horses. They could be folded flat and were lighter and easier to transport than metal buckets. When they were soaked, the fibres in the canvas swelled, making them watertight. This example was made in 1939 by the Government Harness and Saddlery Factory at Cawnpore.

Above right: It was a requirement for all British officers serving with Indian regiments to learn Urdu so they could communicate with their men. Many hired a local teacher to help them grasp the basics of the language and the Government of India published books to help the young officer. Urdu was a standardised version of Hindustani and was used as a lingua franca across British India in place of the many dozens of different local languages and dialects of the subcontinent.

brass shoulder titles of the regiment. The kurta was paired with a loose pair of khaki drill trousers and worn with boots and puttees like British military uniforms. This distinctive dress contrasted with the military in India before the Mutiny, when local troops had been uniformed along European lines. After the Mutiny, there was an increasing 'Indianisation' of uniform lasting throughout the second half of the

One of the greatest innovations in warfare on the North West Frontier was the introduction of armoured cars, made by a number of firms such as Crossley Motors, Guy Motors and Rolls-Royce. This driver wears the typical uniform of a man tasked to work with these machines. His overalls are made in India and are a plain khaki cotton design to protect him both from snagging within the vehicle and from oil and dirt when servicing the armoured car. He wears the solar pith helmet and is armed with a .455 Webley revolver. This is carried in an Indian Pattern leather pistol case which, with the leather ammunition pouch, was attached to the pattern 1908 belt with brass hooks. The weapon was a last ditch protection if he ever needed to bail out of the vehicle in an emergency, but it had proven its worth in saving crew members on a number of occasions and so was standard issue to drivers. Around his neck he wears a pair of general purpose goggles to protect his eyes from dust.

The Newbold 'General Purpose' goggles for tank, transport and dispatch riders were some of the most common goggles in use between the wars and were essential when many vehicles lacked windscreens to keep dust out of a man's eyes. This pair can be dated by the grey cloth and fur around the eye pieces as well as the use of all-elastic straps, which were modified in the Second World War to save rubber. They were issued with a metal tin to protect them when not being worn.

nineteenth century, with the increasing adoption of turbans, pantaloons and flowing uniforms. Not only were these more practical for fighting in the subcontinent, but they also preserved 'the distinction between the different nationalities and races, which is very necessary for [British] security.' Until the First World War, Indian troops had paid for their own uniforms, but by the end of the war, uniforms were given out as a free incentive to recruitment and this clearly impressed one sepoy, who remarked that 'if a sepoy chooses, he can get as much clothing as he likes. If he wears out four pairs of boots a week, he can do so. But no one takes any account of these admirable and expensive things. It is as if the government had resolved to think nothing of expense.'

Special pistol equipment was designed to be compatible with the pattern 1908 webbing set for other ranks armed with a pistol. The original pattern consisted of an open-topped leather holster used to carry the Webley revolver. In India a different pattern was developed featuring a cover secured by a closure strap (*left*). This Indian pattern is frequently seen being carried by British troops serving in the subcontinent during the 1930s. In 1935, the Army introduced a new pistol case made in webbing to replace the leather designs (*right*). Both cases shown have 3-inch hooks for attachment to the 1908 belt as well as a sleeve on the rear for a cleaning rod. A pistol ammunition pouch with belt hooks is seen in the centre. Also shown are the small cardboard boxes in which revolver ammunition was issued, each typically containing twelve rounds. The early 1930s saw a change in military policy, as the old .455 calibre revolver was supplanted by a new smaller and lighter model in .380 calibre. The box on the left is for the older, heavier rounds, while that on the right is for the new calibre. Although the new lighter rounds lacked the stopping power of the old ammunition, it was easier to teach a man how to fire the new pattern of revolver with its lighter recoil than the old 'manstopper' cartridge.

In 1928, Guy Motors supplied the Indian Army with over a hundred six-wheel armoured cars. Unlike other models that were based on civilian car chassis, this design was based on a commercial lorry's chassis and was larger and more robust. The design used the same turret design as contemporary Crossley armoured cars, mounting twin machine guns in its dome. The cars sported distinctive circular blower-type radiators and carried spare wheels and sand channels to allow them to be extracted from soft terrain if they bogged down.

As well as these dull khaki service uniforms, Indian soldiers were well known for the range and beauty of their dress uniforms. Each Indian regiment had its own traditional ceremonial wear and colours, which could range from the red of the Viceroy's bodyguard to the canary yellow of the men of Skinner's Horse. The higher the rank, the more elaborate these uniforms became, with officers' tunics being made of a fine and light wool, embellished with lace, frogging and ornate buttons. The uniforms of the Indian other ranks were not usually so opulent, but still displayed the colour that was so reminiscent of the East. Normally, most units only wore these uniforms for special occasions, but some units that were more ceremonial in nature, such as the aforementioned Viceroy's bodyguard, would have worn their dress uniforms almost continually. Kitchener had remarked before the First World War, 'some military display is necessary in an oriental country. If the Amir of Afghanistan came to India, our troops in khaki would not impress him as much as if they were [dressed in] red.'

For British soldiers, the prescribed headdress for wear in India was a sun helmet, either of the earlier Wolseley or the later Solar Topee design. The topee was seen as essential for health in the tropics in the 1930s and Woodbines' book of useful hints for soldiers in India warned, 'Don't go into the blazing sun without your Topee or Helmet, whether it be in Summer or Winter time, the summer especially, between the hours of 9-a.m. and 5-p.m.' The book went on to recommend that 'a few leaves, especially

All soldiers had a wash roll to hold the everyday essentials they needed to keep themselves clean and smart in the field. This example is typical of those used in India between the wars and has a mixture of British and Indian-produced items. The roll contains spare leather shoe laces, knife, fork, spoon, comb, toothbrush, button stick and shaving equipment. The brass button stick was used to protect the uniform from polish whilst cleaning brass buttons and is dated 1933 with an Indian Broad Arrow. On the end of the wash roll is a General Service Mk II pocket watch, 1938-dated jack knife, dubbin to waterproof boots and a selection of Indian coins.

The housewife, also often called a 'hussif', was a small sewing kit that was used by soldiers to maintain their uniform. Typical contents included spare buttons, thread, needles, thimble, wool for darning socks and cotton for simple repairs, all contained in a small fabric wallet. Tropical uniforms had removable buttons, held on with split rings, as well as removable brass belt hooks. As both of these were easily lost, spares were often carried in the hussif. Note the brass general service button in the foreground that is marked as having been made in Simla, India, and the two shirt buttons, each with a manufacturer's mark for Abdul Aleem and a date of 1934.

Neem leaves, placed inside the Topee when in the jungle will keep the head cool.' Sun helmets made of sola pith, known as Cawnpore helmets, had been in service since the 1890s unofficially and were covered in khaki drill, often with a quilted pattern. They were initially used for fatigue duties to preserve the more expensive cork Wolseley pattern helmets from damage. It was found that helmets made of sola pith were lighter and more comfortable to wear than the Wolseley pattern and they quickly became the preferred design for use on campaign. Sola pith comes from a flowering aquatic plant, *Aeschynomene aspera*, indigenous to India and other parts of South-East Asia, mostly in areas that flood seasonally such as rice paddies. The helmet was shaped from this sola pith and then covered in a removable cotton drill cover to protect the basic helmet. In 1938, the 'Hat, Pith, Khaki, Solar' was officially adopted, replacing both the quilted Cawnpore helmets and the Wolseley pattern, although examples of the latter continued to be produced until around 1943 with both designs in service concurrently.

Above left: The company that manufactured Wild Woodbine cigarettes produced a guide for ordinary soldiers heading to India for the first time between the wars. The book offered simple advice on health, currency and recreation in the subcontinent and gave some cultural background that would have been helpful to troops leaving for the first time to go abroad.

Above right: Police-type whistles were issued to officers and NCOs as a method of communicating simple orders to their troops above the noise of battle. This example was procured by the Indian Army, as indicated by the Broad Arrow over an 'I' acceptance stamp marked into the body of the whistle. While the Indian Army imported many items and added their acceptance mark, this is an Indian-made example produced by Bharadwaj & Co. of Aligarh in the United Provinces in 1938.

This Mk V Outfit Anti-Dimming bears the
Indian Army acceptance mark and appears to
have been produced in India itself. The finish
is cruder than examples made in the United
Kingdom and it lacks the printed instructions
that can be found on British examples. One
end has a cloth for applying the anti-dimming
paste, while the other has the paste itself;
the red band allows the user to differentiate
between the two. The date of manufacture,
1939, is impressed into one of the screw caps.

The 'hat, pith, khaki, solar' was officially
introduced in 1938, though it had been used for
active service much earlier. This pattern had a
four-panel construction with a flat top and thick
brim and four ventilation grommets were often
present. A puggaree or simple band was used, in
this case with a flash for the Devonshire Regiment
affixed. The inset showing the paper label indicates
that this helmet was made by the Peninsular Hat
Manufacturing Company of Calcutta in 1938
and shows an Indian Army acceptance stamp in
black ink.

Indian troops often wore turbans, with different designs indicating the different ethnic backgrounds of the men. Sikhs wore their traditional turban made up of many yards of cloth called a pagri, carefully wound around the head, but without any form of central cone. Many Muslim soldiers, however, wound their pagri around a stiffened conical headpiece called a khulla. Originally this had been made of wicker or straw

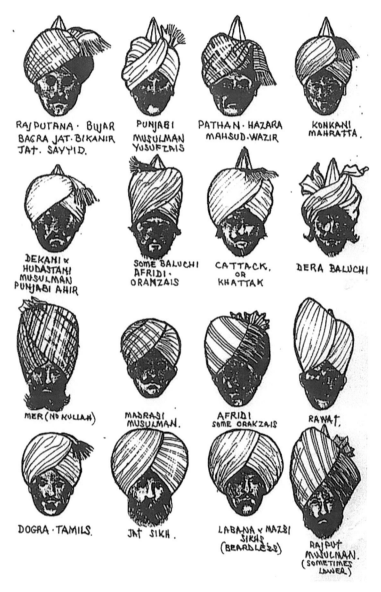

This drawing from the period shows some of the wide variety of turbans that could be found among the soldiers of the Indian Army between the wars. It was possible to tell the ethnic origins of a particular soldier from the style of his turban, with many regional traditions being closely followed.

covered in cloth, but by this period it was made purely of quilted cloth. These turbans often included a coloured piece of cloth called a shamla in the top of the turban to help identify which unit a man was from. The ethnographers of the period took great interest in these variations, recording them and the different looks preferred by different ethnic groupings. The dense fabric of the turban acted much like a helmet and many Sikh soldiers in the Second World War were to forgo a steel helmet in favour of their traditional turban. Headdress, like uniforms, varied with khaki drab versions being used on a day-to-day basis, and more elaborate and colourful headdress used for more formal and ceremonial occasions. These turbans were time-consuming to wrap smartly and correctly, so they were usually removed as a single piece in the manner of a hat, rather than being completely disassembled and rewound each time a man needed to put them on.

Webbing equipment in India was the usual mixture of 1908 pattern Mills webbing for the infantry and leather bandolier equipment for artillery and mounted troops. Limited production of both sets does seem to have taken place in India itself, with Indian-made examples of 1908 pattern webbing and bandoliers marked as having been produced by the Government Harness and Saddlery Factory, Cawnpore, occasionally being seen on the collector's market. The vast majority of this equipment, however, was manufactured in Great Britain and shipped out to the subcontinent. The 1908 pattern equipment was subject to a few modifications during the interwar period. In 1921, the water bottle carrier's securing strap was modified, switching from a long strap with a front closure to two shorter straps fastened with a press stud on the top shoulder of the bottle. Brass eyelets were added to the weather flaps of the pack in 1922. Then, in 1923, the British Army declared the entrenching tool obsolete, along with its webbing head and helve carriers. Accordingly, the helve carrier attachment strap on the bayonet frog was deleted in 1924. The 1903 bandolier equipment had technically been made obsolete by the introduction of the innovative 1908 pattern webbing just five years after it was introduced. Despite this fact, it continued to be manufactured and worn well into the Second World War. The simple bandolier was ideal for cavalry and troops who were not expected to need the large amount of ammunition of an infantryman. The bandolier worn on its own was easy to carry and held fifty rounds of ammunition securely without intruding on the wearer's waist, which was ideal for those moving around on horseback or operating an artillery piece. Likewise, the belt, a bayonet frog and two fifteen-round ammunition pouches were ideal for ceremonial troops, being light enough to be worn for extended periods of time while not interfering with drill movements, yet still giving the soldier some ammunition if an incident were to occur.

British other ranks were largely kept apart from the local population, and apart from a few parades, life in India was not usually very arduous. As an outlet for their energies, great store was placed in sports and regular sporting matches were held with sections competing against each other regularly, with more prestigious competitions arranged between different regiments. Exercise was felt to be good for the soldier's health and a period guide advised, 'exercise is more necessary in India than England. It keeps the liver active and circulation in order, but should not be continued long

Above left: This cavalryman from the 16th The Queen's Lancers prepares for the regiment's final parade in Lucknow in 1922 before his regiment merges with the 5th Royal Irish Lancers on 11 April. He wears the khaki drill service dress jacket with cord breeches, this heavyweight fabric being more robust and better suited to cavalrymen, who spent most of their days in the saddles of their horses. On his head he wears the service dress cap with the brass cap badge of his regiment. His puttees are wrapped in the 'cavalry' fashion, from the top of the calf to the ankle with the tape at the bottom of the puttee rather than at the top. He carries the pattern 1908 cavalry sword. This design had a tapering 35-inch blade, blackened for use in combat, and had a composite pistol grip hilt with a large protective sheet steel bowl guard to protect the cavalryman's hand.

Above right: As a cavalryman, this soldier wears the nine-pocket version of the 1903 leather bandolier. Unlike the standard pattern that held fifty rounds in five pockets across the chest, this design added an extra four pockets across the back, bringing the total capacity up to ninety rounds. Over his boots he wears a pair of spurs, secured with brown leather straps that incorporate a lace protector. The disc at the rear of the spur was known as a rowel and the spikes on this were quite small and blunt on British Army-issued examples, to prevent an inexperienced rider from injuring the horse.

enough as to cause exhaustion.' For physical training, men were issued with the same sort of long shorts and long-sleeved rugby shirts as were used for playing games in Britain at the period. For regimental teams, a separate kit was often provided in the regiment's colours, paid for with mess funds. A regiment's sporting prowess was lauded in regimental journals and team photographs.

Food was a constant thought in men's minds and one soldier serving in India from the Royal Scots opined, 'all the years I remained in the ranks, I spent the whole of my money to provide myself with enough food to prevent malnutrition.' This is certainly an exaggeration, but the truth remains that British soldiers were always on the lookout for ways to supplement their rations. Until 1927, many military camps and cantonments in India were serviced by the Indian Army Canteen Board, who ran cheap restaurants for the men and small shops where they could purchase subsidised goods and avoid being cheated by unscrupulous merchants. The Canteen Board was liquidated in 1927 under somewhat shady circumstances and replaced by individual contractors, who bid for the rights to supply troops on a camp-by-camp basis.

Although life in India, apart from the frontier, was largely peaceful between the wars, there were a number of local incidents that grew to such a size as to become full-scale insurrections and which required the deployment of sizeable numbers of troops to restore order. The most significant of these was the Malabar or Moplah Rebellion in southern India between 1921 and 1922. This region of India was largely agrarian with land owned by Hindus of the Brahmin or Nayar castes and largely cultivated by Muslim tenants called the Moplahs or Mappillas. Although the region was predominantly Hindu, up to a third of the peasantry was Moplah and their numbers were increasing as low-caste Hindus converted to Islam. Tensions of class, power and religion were endemic in the region with minor incidents occurring for many centuries, the Moplahs typically burning and looting farms, destroying Hindu temples and then mounting a last stand in a fortified building such as a mosque.

The rebellion that broke out in the aftermath of the First World War was rather different, however, as tensions increased at the same time Britain was introducing a more representative scheme of local government through the Government of India Act, which encouraged Indian nationalism and made the Imperial government appear far weaker than it had at any point since the end of the Mutiny. In 1921, open rebellion broke out with the Moplah peasantry attacking Hindu properties and shops. As law and order collapsed, the region was divided up into 'rebel kingdoms' while groups of brigands patrolled the roads and destroyed telegraph wires to disrupt communications in the district.

There were only thirty soldiers in the region, a detachment of the Leinsters, and there was little they could do to put down the rebellion in its early stages. Moreover, the civil administration was loath to repeat the mistakes of Amritsar that loomed large in its members' consciousness, having occurred only a couple of years before. In this state of paralysis, religious violence broke out on an unprecedented scale with heinous atrocities being carried out upon the Hindu population of the region. Murder, rape and

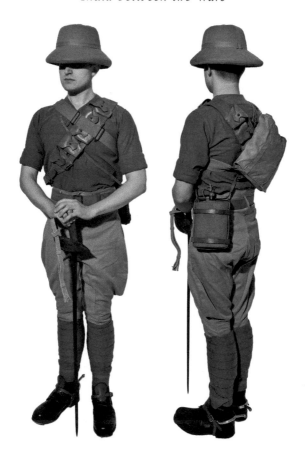

Above left: Cavalry retained its importance in India throughout the interwar period. Full mechanisation was a slow and expensive process and the open plains of India still lent themselves very well to cavalry operations. The ordinary cavalryman's uniform continued to develop in this period. The most obvious indicator that this cavalryman dates from the 1930s is his 'hat, pith, khaki, solar' or sun helmet, which only saw widespread use in the later decade. The cavalry sword this trooper is leaning on is the pattern 1908, introduced before the outbreak of the First World War. The sword was designed for thrusting and was only used in a charge. Due to its lack of any other function, the scabbard was mounted on the saddle as it was felt to be of no use to a dismounted man.

Above right: The carrying of a respirator haversack was problematic for mounted troops. The usual position on the chest was unsuitable as it obstructed a rider from controlling his horse safely. The proscribed place to carry the haversack was on the back, over one shoulder. This kept the haversack out of the way, but allowed it to be quickly swung round to the front to allow the respirator to be worn if a gas attack did come. The older Mk I.T. haversack used in the early interwar period had to be modified by cutting and resewing the tabs that held the sling, in order to be worn in this manner. The later Mk V respirator haversack, shown here, was designed to be easily reconfigured from the infantry arrangement. The water bottle is carried in a leather 'other services' carrier. This design had been introduced in 1901 and although commonly associated with the cavalry, was also used by others who were not issued infantry-style webbing equipment. The leather carrying strap had a canvas flare where it passed over the shoulder to improve comfort for the wearer.

forced conversion were all commonplace and it was clear that the authorities would have to react.

The rebels tried to ambush a column of British troops and police in August 1921. Despite the column being just 170 men and the rebels numbering over 3,000, the Moplahs suffered heavily, losing 300 men from charging machine-gun positions alone. In the wake of this defeat the rebels melted away and adopted classic insurgency tactics instead, relying on concealment in the local jungle and employing hit-and-run attacks.

To counter this development, the British deployed large numbers of troops and declared martial law in the area. Military commanders had far more limited powers than was usually the case, however, and suppressing the rebellion was a far harder and lengthier job. Further reinforcements were sent to the region in September 1921, but suppressing the rebellion was still difficult.

> The rebel leaders now avoid open conflict with the troops and have adopted guerrilla warfare, ambushing and sniping columns, re-occupying places which the troops have passed, looting, terrorising and forcibly converting all inhabitants of other persuasions, commandeering crops and food supplies and destroying property and communications.

In October 1921, the British changed tactics and a sweep was arranged across the whole region running from the north-west to the south-east. The Ghurkhas, a company

Sport was an important part of life in India, giving a healthy outlet for men's energy. Formal competitions were set up between regimental teams at the larger military camps in India and men were enthusiastically supported by their regimental colleagues. Impressive trophies could be purchased by mail order and awarded to the winning team, such as this trophy won by the 2nd Dorsetshire Regiment in the Madras Gymkhana Football Cup in 1920.

A plate and cutlery marked to the Indian Army Canteen Board. This organisation provided subsidised meals to soldiers across India from 1913 until it was disbanded in 1927. The badge of the Canteen Board is marked on all items and consists of an elephant within an oval surmounted by an oriental-style crown.

of the Dorsetshire Regiment and a detachment of armoured cars pushed the rebels onto a waiting line of troops that killed or captured many. This was followed up by an assault on a fortified house in which many rebels were hiding, requiring the use of mountain howitzers to force them out. The official report declared:

> This was the most serious blow the insurgents had so far received, nearly 250 Moplahs being accounted for, without any British casualties, while four days later the Malapuram and Perintalmanna garrisons co-operated most successfully against another large party and inflicted nearly 50 casualties on it, without suffering any losses themselves.

By November, rebels were surrendering en masse and the movement fizzled out, allowing peace to be restored. The campaign highlighted both the difficulties of fighting in wooded terrain and the utility of armoured cars in forcing insurgents out of hiding.

4

North West Frontier

For the aspiring British Army officer between the wars, there was arguably no place he would rather be stationed than the North West Frontier Province of India. Here the ambitious subaltern was almost guaranteed to see combat at some point in his tour against the local tribesmen who called the region home. Throughout the interwar period low-level tribal warfare was endemic, with occasional bouts of full-scale warfare breaking out. Possession of the region was seen as vital as the Frontier, along with the independent country of Afghanistan, provided a buffer between Imperial India and Russia. Anglo-Russian tensions in the region dated back to the nineteenth century, but in the interwar period these tensions were also coloured by a deep mistrust of the new Bolshevik regime. The Indian Government was worried that the message of Bolshevism would be added to the religious tensions within the country and lead to open rebellion, and even the overthrow of British rule in India. In this atmosphere, it remained crucial to keep the peace in the area to help maintain that distance from the Russian Bear.

The First World War might have been over in Europe, but 1919 saw the start of a new wave of fighting along the North West Frontier of India with the Raj under pressure from both its northern neighbour Afghanistan and the fiercely independent tribesmen of the region. In February 1919 the Amir of Afghanistan was murdered and his successor, Amanullah, sought to gain complete independence from the British Empire by invading India. British India was still suffering the results of a manpower crisis in the wake of the First World War and political unrest further south in the subcontinent. After fierce but localised fighting, an armistice was agreed upon and in return for the removal of British influence in her foreign affairs, Afghanistan agreed to respect the Durrand Line and the Third Afghan War was brought to a conclusion. Needless to say, local tribesmen ignored this border and crossed it at will throughout the period, quickly recognising that the British would not violate the border and so ensuring their own safety by crossing into Afghan territory when threatened by British and Indian forces.

The North West Frontier was a particularly rugged landscape in which to carry out operations, with the region characterised by high mountains, deep passes and narrow defiles that made European-style warfare very difficult and tribal ambushes easy. The British tried to rule this region with a light touch, letting the tribesmen rule themselves for the most part as long as they did not interfere with regional commerce, ferment violence or attack British outposts. Tribes were paid a stipend from the Government of

Above left: The North West Frontier of India needed a permanent military presence in one form or another for the entire length of British rule in India. Extra troops were dispatched to the region in periods of tension, such as this private who has recently arrived as part of the build-up of forces during the Third Afghan War to prevent any possibility of the local tribesmen taking advantage of the ongoing conflict. The private is dressed in late First World War tropical equipment with pattern 1908 webbing worn over a khaki drill service dress jacket and shorts. Of note is the distinctive style of wrapping the puttees, with a twist having been introduced to the front of a few wraps as the size increases from ankle to calf. Besides adding a small feature of decoration, this gave the puttees a smarter appearance and a more secure fit.

Above right: Although fitting instructions directed that the pattern 1908 haversack be worn low with the weight taken by the belt, soldiers are often seen wearing it high on the shoulders for a smarter appearance. There is also a rolled groundsheet attached to the back of the belt with the support straps. This groundsheet offered a waterproof surface on which to sleep in the open, and could be used as an improvised poncho to protect the wearer from rain while on the march. Two of the sheets could be tied together to make a small two-man shelter.

India for good behaviour and, equally, were fined for recalcitrance and open defiance. Unfortunately for the British, the tribesmen of this region obeyed their own code of honour and to British eyes were frequently treacherous. The frontier tribesmen did not recognise the border between India and Afghanistan and there was a constant danger that a charismatic religious leader would encourage them into open rebellion.

The North West Frontier was characterised by high mountains and narrow passes, making it a particularly challenging territory in which to fight. Ambushes were commonplace and the rebellious nature of the tribesmen in the region caused problems for the British throughout the period. Hill forts were built on strategic outcrops to help protect the few passable roads in the region from bandits and tribal incursions.

The Indian Government Ammunition Factory, Kirkee, started manufacturing .303 ammunition in 1895 and would continue to do so for the next sixty-five years. This packet contains ten rounds of .303 ball ammunition, manufactured in 1939 at the factory. The rounds are wrapped in a paper packet tied with a piece of string. Details of the rounds are stamped in green ink on the outside, including the type of round and the load date.

The khaki-coloured service uniform was occasionally used as the basis for ceremonial wear. This subadar-major of the 8th Punjabis wears a dress uniform that, although khaki, features elaborate frogging across the chest and blue facings on the cuffs and collars. This is worn with a dress cross belt and medals along with a brightly coloured turban.

Policing the Frontier was a difficult and expensive business. Throughout this period, the British tried to find ways to reduce their expenditure with the application of new technology that was seen as a way of supporting and, in some cases, supplanting traditional infantry tactics. While trials had taken place with First World War-era tanks in the region, these lacked the mobility needed on the frontier and were still expensive and difficult to maintain. It would only be the development of light tanks in the late 1920s that finally saw a tracked vehicle that was swift enough and cheap enough to be effective come into service. The armoured car, however, was ideally suited for warfare on the North West Frontier and in this period most were either Rolls-Royce or the more numerous Crossley models. These vehicles were made using the heavy-duty chassis provided by the manufacturer, to which a light armoured body was attached with a turret on the top, which usually mounted one or two Vickers medium machine guns. The Rolls-Royce design was more powerful than the Crossley cars, but both were ideally suited to warfare on the Frontier. The men who drove the cars would also have to maintain them in the field and make repairs if they broke down to allow them to return to their bases. As such, it was common for the crew of armoured cars to wear protective one-piece overalls with the ubiquitous sun helmet and goggles to protect their eyes from the pervasive dust that was such a feature of India.

The designs had been developed before the First World War, but came into their own on the Frontier where they could act as mobile pill boxes, traversing the roads of the region and virtually impervious to the rifle fire of the tribesmen. They were also cheaper to purchase than tanks and could be easily maintained by any motor mechanic. Modifications made to them for service in India included fitting rifle loopholes on the turret bevels to allow rifle fire to be directed upwards into the passes at tribesmen firing down on the cars, the fitting of Raybestos (a woven asbestos) to the interior of the vehicles to reduce the heat inside the cars and a domed turret that seems to have been specially designed for India, as it was not seen anywhere else in the Empire. This had four firing positions with quick-release mounts, allowing the two machine guns to be remounted in about 15 seconds in an alternative position to better deal with threats.

While highly effective, armoured cars were not invulnerable. Simple road blocks of boulders across a road could effectively halt an armoured car, leaving it open for ambush as the crew attempted to clear the rocks. They were also particularly unsuited to operations inside some of the more built-up cities of the region. In April 1930, disorder broke out in Peshawar City as part of the wider Red Shirt movement in the region. This was a rebellion in the North West Frontier province amongst the Pathan tribesmen, fomented by a radical preacher called Abdul Ghafar Khan, which sought complete independence and unity between Hindus and Muslims. His followers dressed in red shirts, giving the rebellion its distinctive name. Although initially peaceful, the government viewed the movement as seditious after a number of agitators were arrested and rioting and violence broke out in Peshawar City. To assist the civil power, troops were dispatched with four armoured cars from No. 2 Section, No. 1 Armoured Car Company. Peshawar City is built on a series of hills with steep narrow streets containing tall, overhanging buildings that made operations particularly difficult and unsuited for armoured cars. Nevertheless, the four cars, *Bray*, *Bullicourt*, *Bethune* and *Bapaume*, were

Cigarette cases were often purchased as gifts and could be engraved with personal messages. This case reads, 'To my brother Will ~ With best wishes ~ From Sgt. George Goodswen ~ R.A.F. India.'

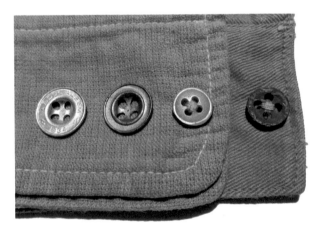

A selection of Indian-produced buttons for uniforms. Left to right: Aluminium, galvanised iron, horn/bone and coconut shell. Buttons had been produced in India as a craft industry for centuries, but the two biggest suppliers of coconut shell buttons to the Army were the Janda Manufacturing Company and the International Manufacturing Company, both of Lahore.

ordered into the city. Accounts vary of the events that followed, but the official British report states that when the cars entered they were pelted with improvised missiles and they closed down to protect their crews. A motorcycle rider who accompanied the cars was pulled from his bike and killed by the mob, prompting the crew of *Bullicourt* to move forward to protect his body, knocking over some of the crowd in the process and enraging them further. The mob then attacked the armoured cars with crowbars and axes and finally produced some petrol which they used to set alight the body of the despatch rider and the *Bethune*. The crew escaped from their blazing vehicle and managed to make their way to the *Bray*, using their revolvers to protect themselves from the mob. Fighting continued for the rest of the day and the armoured cars had to pull back.

Tactically, this incident showed some of the vulnerabilities of the cars when operating in tightly packed streets with large, densely congregated crowds. Desperately trying to avoid another massacre like Amritsar, the armoured cars did not use their machine guns and, in effect, became static pillboxes, which allowed them to become trapped in the narrow streets where rioters could get close enough to physically attack them and set fire to one. The official history of operations noted:

> Armoured cars should not be used unsupported by infantry or police, to push back a crowd by moving slowly against it. If they are to be used to clear away a mob, infantry should move in support of the cars to block side roads. It is a general principle that cars must be kept on the move when in the neighbourhood of a mob and that very narrow streets and defiles should be avoided.

From 1931, the armoured units began to convert to light tanks, although armoured cars remained in widespread use until the outbreak of the Second World War.

The second emerging technology that the British took advantage of in northern India was that of airpower. Although less than twenty years old, the First World War had allowed the aeroplane to become a tried and proven weapon of war and the newly created Royal Air Force argued that the use of aircraft was an effective and cheap way of policing tribal regions. Airfields were established at Peshawar, Kohat, Arawali, Risalpur, Miranshah and Quetta, with advanced landing strips prepared nearer to the tribal regions as required. The aircraft in use during the interwar period included Bristol F2Bs and de Havilland DH9s from 1919 until 1929, when Westland Wapitis entered service. Flying aircraft on the Frontier was far from straightforward, with weather being a constant problem: heavy snow blocking airstrips in the winter, hot arid conditions swirling up dust in the summer and flooding in the rainy season were all natural hazards that had to be overcome. During the 1930s, the Indian Government cut the budget to the RAF, with the resulting drop in aircraft availability allowing the army to claim that the conditions on the Frontier were fundamentally unsuited to air operations. Inter-service rivalry was common between the two forces throughout this period.

Once the decision was made that a tribe needed to be punished for some transgression and that air power was deemed the most effective method, an aircraft flew over the village that was to be targeted and leaflets were dropped outlining when and where a bombing would take place. This gave time for the tribesmen to remove themselves, their families and their livestock. Then, at the appointed hour, the RAF returned and dropped bombs on the buildings of a village, setting fire to them and razing the settlement. With honour satisfied, the tribesmen then returned and began rebuilding the village, hopefully suitably chastened for the foreseeable future. Other uses included dispersing tribal gatherings before they had time to coalesce into an open rebellion; in 1927, the RAF dispersed a tribal lashkar of Mohmands who had fired on British troops with bombing and air-to-ground strafing.

During more serious incidents, the preliminary warning was dropped and a straightforward bombing run was carried out. In 1923, the authorities were having trouble with the Ahmedzai-Wazirs in Waziristan and thirty-seven bombing sorties were undertaken in April as punishment for what the official history euphemistically calls 'outrages'. In the course of these sorties it was estimated that fifty tribesmen were killed or injured, and large numbers of livestock killed. Livestock represented one of the few material resources of the tribesmen, so their loss was a particularly effective punishment. While highly effective as a punitive measure, air power was recognised as having its limitations as early as the 1930s. Unfriendly tribesmen, if they knew an air attack was imminent, hid in the villages of tribes known to be friendly to the British. There was little the authorities could do to extract them from the air when this was the case. It was also recognised that there was a need to foster good relations with tribes, rather than just punishing bad behaviour. It was felt that building roads and increasing the activities of political officers and infantry was a more effective method and a contemporary report noted:

> The only real solution of the Frontier tribal problem is development and assistance on the road to civilisation. Two of the chief aids to that are good communications and free intercourse. Any innovations on the military side, whether in the direction of exercising control by air or by any other means, should have in view these requirements, and cater for them.

It is also notable that by the later interwar period, the British and Indian authorities were beginning to question the morality of bombing tribesmen from the air and the potential public outcry in both Britain and India towards methods that were seen as being unfair.

For all these technical innovations, warfare on the frontier remained much as it had been for the last century, with a need for infantry on the ground. Despite their largely 'hands off' approach to policing the territory, the British did maintain a number of large camps from which operations could be launched. The two largest of these were at Landi Kotal and on the plateau at Razmak. Both camps started out as large tented establishments surrounded by a perimeter of barbed wire, but as they became more established, permanent buildings were constructed and British Indian Army officer Francis Ingall recalled:

> Apart from the military cantonment, Landi Kotal comprised a fort, a caravanserai or inn to accommodate travellers with the camel trains, and of course the railway station. The cantonment housed two infantry battalions, one British and one Indian, as well as a mountain battery, a brigade HQ and several ancillary units including a joint (British and Indian) hospital. The third battalion of the brigade, usually Ghurkhas, held the frontier post five miles away at Landi Khana, on the frontier with Afghanistan.
>
> In my day the camp was not a very aesthetic picture, but it was compact: row upon row of neatly spaced mud-walled barracks with corrugated iron roofs. As Landi Kotal stands on a high plateau the winters here were bitterly cold and these corrugated iron roofs provided very little insulation from the weather, allowing the cold to penetrate in winter and acting as a griddle during the searing heat of summer. The camp was enclosed within a triple barbed-wire apron with defensive posts sited at tactical intervals and gates that were normally kept locked. Outside the gates was the area of the fort and just beyond the

perimeter to the east lay an emergency landing ground. The gates were manned by day and all local people needed a pass to enter, but at night the various posts were also manned, with searchlights playing upon the terrain outside the barbed wire. Anyone approaching the camp was challenged and if he didn't respond he would be fired upon. The fort itself was small and out of date; it played no part in the cantonment's defences.

Typically, small groups of men were sent out from the camps to defend outposts, with company-sized forays used to police the region. As an infantry force, the British and Indian troops were largely equipped in the same manner as infantry across the Empire, with the 1908 pattern webbing seeing service throughout the period. Despite this, some unique alterations to the way it was worn were adopted by troops on the Frontier to reflect the nature of the fighting they were involved in. Water bottles were routinely moved from the right side of the set to the small of the back and were loosely fastened by the buckles so they could be more easily detached when the soldier needed a drink. It was recognised that hydration was essential for soldiers in the heat of India and simple changes helped to improve the British soldier's efficiency in the field. Other modifications included carrying a waterproof groundsheet or cape, tucked through the webbing support straps on the rear of the set. Although the region was predominantly hot and dry, flash rain storms were a possibility, and at night temperatures could fall rapidly. A blanket wrapped in a waterproof cape was a simple way of carrying both bedding for sleeping in the open at night and protection if the weather were to turn inclement.

Landi Kotal camp in the North West Frontier Province was a large military encampment consisting of barrack blocks, a hospital, church, parade ground and other essential buildings. It was surrounded by a perimeter fence of barbed wire and fortified gatehouses. The rugged landscape of the region is visible, with a natural plateau providing the only space on which a camp of this size could be built. Accommodation was always at a premium so canvas tents supplemented the more permanent buildings.

Above left: In November 1936 it was agreed to send troops into the Lower Khaisora Valley in the North West Frontier Province to expel a troublesome faqir from the Tori Khel tribal region. Unfortunately, the Tori Khel rose up against the Raj instead, and it was necessary to send a punitive expedition in December of 1936. The majority of infantry troops in Waziristan at this time were from Indian Army regiments; however, this private is from the 1st Battalion Hampshire Regiment. He is dressed in the typical uniform of British regiments on campaign in the province in the late 1930s. He wears on his head the 'hat, pith, khaki, solar', which had largely replaced the old Wolseley pattern on campaign by this point. His shirt is a collarless design made of wool with a cotton collar band, which was commonly rolled inside the shirt. Epaulettes have been added to the shirt, a common modification made by men serving on the North West Frontier. He wears the pattern 1908 web equipment and his SMLE is fitted with a 'sling, rifle, pattern 1914', which was still in limited service at this point.

Above right: From the rear, it can be seen that this soldier is wearing his equipment in the style favoured on the Frontier: the pack is worn in rucksack style with the supporting straps used as improvised shoulder straps, allowing the pack to be dropped quickly if contact was made with the enemy. He also wears his water bottle in its cradle on the back of the belt to leave him unencumbered for easier movement in the rugged landscape of the province. He has also opted to replace the high puttees seen earlier in the period with shorter ankle-length examples.

The Wolseley pattern sun helmet originated in the late nineteenth century and continued in service with the British Army throughout the interwar period. This cork helmet had a distinctive brim with a pointed front and flat downward-sweeping back, which offered greater sun protection to the neck. The puggaree was reduced in size and number of folds throughout the period, with this 1932 example having the earlier thick style with nine folds.

One innovation of the khaki solar pith hat was the removable khaki drill cover, which could be replaced or washed if soiled. The cover was held in place with a drawstring and a couple of stitches on the band and top ventilation cap. Note how the sweatband is permanently sewn in place on this type of helmet.

Another common change was to attach the supporting straps to the large pack in such a manner as to allow it to be worn as a rucksack, the thin straps being tucked into the open side of a pair of Twigg buckles on the shoulder braces. This prevented the rucksack from slipping off the shoulders unintentionally, and it only took moments to unhook it and let it fall to the ground if a man needed to fight unencumbered.

The standard pattern 1908 webbing set was worn universally by both British and Indian infantrymen on the North West Frontier during the interwar period. When fighting in this region of India, it was typical for men to wear the water bottle centrally on the rear of the waistband, held in place by the gated side of the carrier's Twigg buckles (*left inset*). This allowed the bottle and carrier to be quickly removed for a drink during rest stops in a way that the official method did not allow. Note the Mk VI water bottle in its thinner serge cloth cover, introduced in 1933. These new covers were a greener shade of khaki than the felt covers, but continued to be sewn directly to the 18-inch stopper cord. On the Frontier, the haversack was frequently dropped in favour of the large pack. With its larger capacity, this was well suited to sustained operations and could carry three or four times the amount of the much smaller haversack. One change made to the large pack in 1922 was the fitting of a pair of brass eyelets to the two side flaps, allowing them to be tied together with a piece of string. A widespread change to the method of wearing the large pack involved carrying the pack rucksack-style, using the support straps as shoulder straps. This allowed the pack to be easily slipped off when contact was made with the enemy. The two support straps were hooked into the open gates of the sliding Twigg buckles on the braces (*right inset*); this prevented them from slipping off the shoulder or digging into the wearer's axilla.

Uniform again largely followed standard practice; however, men often wore a simple collarless shirt with khaki drill shorts, supplemented with a woollen sweater and greatcoat as the temperatures dropped in the evening. The mountainous terrain meant that the winters in the North West Frontier could be harsh and in the 1920s one regiment marched into Razmak camp in their greatcoats in the teeth of a gale and blizzard. Nevertheless, the mountain air did offer exceptionally good visibility when the weather was clear. Here the British had an advantage over the tribesmen, as each unit had a number of signallers. Simple visual signalling like semaphore flags could be seen with a pair of binoculars on a clear day for several miles. The heliograph, however, allowed messages to be sent up to 50 miles and, unlike telegraph wires, it was impossible for tribesmen to cut these messages off. With these forms of communication, the British and Indian troops had a massive tactical advantage and air power or reinforcements could be requested in minutes, rather than the hours it would have taken for a foot messenger to get through. Early wireless and field telephones all supplemented visual signalling and as technology and communications improved across the region, it became easier for the British to police the Frontier.

The heliograph was an instrument that used mirrors to reflect sunlight in order to send messages across long distances. By the interwar period, the 'Heliograph, 5-inch, Mark V' was the most common version in service. It was mounted on a wooden tripod for use and carried separately in a leather case for transport, seen here slung around the tripod. To be used effectively, the heliograph required a clear line of sight. Accordingly, they were well suited to the mountains of the North West Frontier Province, where soaring ridges were commonplace. If the sun was not in a suitable position to hit the main signalling mirror, the second mirror could be angled to bounce the light onto the main reflector. Setting up a heliograph was a skilled job, but it gave the British a tactical advantage over the local tribesmen and allowed messages to be relayed up to 50 miles instantaneously.

The 'Telescope, Signalling (Mk IV) also General Service' was used alongside the heliograph to enhance its range. A man using a telescope could make out the signal from another signalling position over much greater distances than with his eyes alone. It is mounted on a 'Signalling Telescope Stand Mk V', which could be folded up for transport. The leather cups fitted over each end to protect it, with the canvas strap allowing it to be slung over a shoulder.

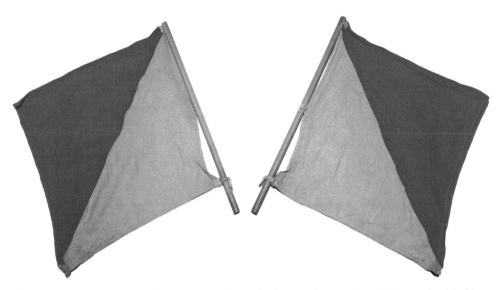

Flags were used to communicate messages through the use of semaphore. This involved holding the arms in different positions, each representing a different letter. Although this could be done with just the arms, it was much easier to read at long distances if large, brightly coloured flags were used. The yellow and red allowed the flags to be visible regardless of the background behind the signaller, with at least one of the two colours likely to be observed.

The Type D Mk III* field telephone had been developed in the First World War and remained in service throughout the interwar period. This field telephone was carried in a sturdy leather case and had the ability to send Morse messages through a built-in buzzer, or to be used for voice communications through the handset. The telephone was powered by two cell batteries and needed a telephone wire to be laid and connected up in order to be used.

Unrest never stopped on the North West Frontier and even after the British left in 1948, the tribesmen continued to show their independent streak, no more wanting to be ruled from Islamabad in Pakistan than they had from Delhi in Imperial India. Even today, the tribal regions remain unstable and it seems unlikely that this will change for many years to come. Combat on the frontier was some of the fiercest a young soldier could expect to encounter in this period, and for young men seeking adventure it was the ideal crucible in which to temper their mettle.

The Vickers-Berthier was a licensed copy of the French Fusil Mitrailleur Berthier Modèle 1922 that was produced by Vickers in their Crayford factory from 1925 onwards. They had hoped to sell it to the British Government as a replacement for the Lewis gun. The British did not adopt the weapon, preferring the Bren gun. The Indian Army did agree to adopt the weapon in 1933 and a production line was set up at the Ishapore Rifle Factory. It was to remain the Indian Army's light machine gun until the Bren gun saw it relegated to second-line use from 1943 onwards. This soldier is demonstrating firing the Vickers-Berthier from the shoulder in the early 1930s and he wears experimental webbing pouches used to carry the curved magazines of the weapon.

Visually, the Vickers Berthier was very similar to the Bren, but parts and fittings were not interchangeable. The Indian Army had special adjustable slings produced for their LMG with a snap hook at either end, and a buckle to adjust the length for comfort. This example was made by the Mills Equipment Company in 1931. The magazines are visually very similar at first glance, sharing the curved shape necessitated by the rimmed .303 round. On closer inspection though there is a distinctive reinforcing rib on the exterior of the Vickers-Berthier magazine.

Hot strong tea has always been appreciated by British soldiers and this Gordon Highlander would have been a welcome sight as he brings up a dixie of the sweetened drink for his comrades. The dixie is a large 3-gallon metal container that acted as stew pot, tea boiler and an effective way of moving food short distances. Throughout the interwar period the Highland regiments continued to wear kilts on active service and this private wears the full kilt of his regiment, made of 9 yards of wool. Over the front of the kilt, he wears a khaki drill kilt apron which protected the expensive garment from damage and dirt. It has a single-buttoned pocket on the front in place of the sporran and secures with two cotton tapes, tied at the rear. The kilt is worn with the grey woollen collarless shirt, commonly known as a 'greyback'. This garment is pulled over the head and has three metal buttons to secure it at the neck as well as a piece of white cotton tape in the centre of the chest where a man's name could be written. This Highlander wears his 1908 webbing in Fatigue Order.

British officers walk down a street of shops in an Indian hill town, possibly Simla. British other ranks were very much restricted on which local shops they could frequent and many were out of bounds. For those shops that they were permitted to visit, the British troops brought welcome income and soldiers were always willing to spend their wages on food, entertainment and female company to relieve the monotony of military life. The street here is particularly wide for an Indian town; however, even from this photograph it is clear how difficult using armoured cars would be in urban areas on steep streets with limited manoeuvrability and tall buildings on either side.

A smaller, flat-topped sun helmet made of sola pith was widely popular with civilians traveling throughout the Empire in the 1920s and 1930s. These helmets were dubbed 'Bombay Bowlers' and were often seen in use by British officers and officials. They had non-removable khaki drill covers and accents like puggarees with many folds and leather top straps, as seen here. This example was distributed by Whiteaway, Laidlaw & Co. Ltd of Calcutta, Bombay, Rangoon, Colombo, Madras, Singapore, Etc., and claims to be 'a protection from sunstroke'.

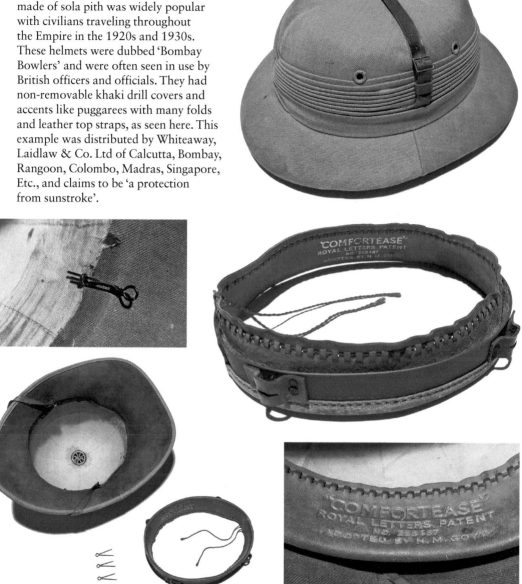

In 1924, Everitt W. Vero & Co. of London patented a new design for sun helmet sweat bands, known as 'Vero's Detachable & Self-Conforming Head Band' or 'Comfortease'. The design comprised a leather sweat band reinforced by a vulcanized fibre band with four slotted brackets that engaged the looped heads of four corresponding pins mounted in the helmet. Split pins were then inserted to hold the sweat band in position, allowing them to be replaced while also increasing ventilation. This pattern became ubiquitous during the interwar years, as it was 'adopted by H. M. Government' and replaced earlier patterns that had the sweat band sewn to cork blocks.

5

The Middle East, Palestine and the League of Nations Mandate

The end of the First World War saw the defeat of the Ottoman Empire in the Middle East by the Allied forces. Although Britain had been involved in Egypt since the late nineteenth century, the lands of Palestine, Iraq and Turkey had been under the control or influence of Constantinople for many centuries. As the Empire tried to deal with conflicting priorities amongst the people of the lands now freed from Ottoman influence, the need to administer this territory, together with internal tensions within Turkey, was to occupy the British Empire throughout the interwar period.

Chanak Crisis

One of the earliest tensions in the region was over the Turkish port of Chanak. The end of the First World War had seen punitive settlements placed upon the Ottomans, and as Turkey emerged from the embers of the former Ottoman Empire she sought to redress some of the aspects of the initial peace terms that she found most egregious. The Dardanelles had been declared a neutral zone between the Greeks and the Turks, who both wished to exert influence over this important shipping lane. The Neutral Zone was maintained by a mixed force of British and French troops and ships. Following their victory over Greek forces in September 1922 with the recapture of Smyrna, the Turks began marching on Constantinople in the neutral zone. The British felt that this was a violation of the original armistice and the British cabinet warned Turkey that any further advances could lead to Great Britain declaring war on the nascent nation. The British forces in the Neutral Zone were centred around the port of Chanak and numbered approximately 27,500 men and a large naval presence. With the addition of French and Italian forces, the Allies could muster around 50,000 men. The Turks numbered just three divisions, but there was little appetite for war amongst the Allies. The French withdrew and agreed to help settle the matter with the Turks, while the British cabinet was firmly split between a small pro-Greek element, led by Lloyd George and Winston Churchill, and the rest of the Conservative coalition, who were pro-Turkish. For the first time Canada refused to automatically support Great Britain if it came to war – a defining moment for the nation, which made it clear to the world that its foreign policy would be decided in Ottawa, not London.

Crisis was averted 2 hours before the British were due to attack the Turks with the signing of an armistice at Mudanya. This ceded the disputed territory of Eastern Thrace to the Turks and would set out the borders between Asia and Europe that have lasted until today. The British military presence in the region is thought to have forced the Turks' hands and brought them to the negotiating table.

The British troops involved in the Chanak Crisis were predominantly drawn from the Royal Navy's Mediterranean fleet with the newly formed 3rd Cruiser Squadron forming the bulk of this force. The squadron consisted of six newly built C-class light cruisers and the Marine detachments aboard each of these ships which, together with the cruisers' 6-inch guns, comprised one of the most potent forces in the region.

Above left: This Royal Marine is part of the British contingent holding the port of Chanak in the Dardanelles Strait in 1922. He wears the white cotton duck uniform for work in the tropics, still in service at the start of the interwar period. This has a single breast pocket on the left-hand side, pointed cuffs and a high standing collar. It is worn with matching trousers and a white Wolseley helmet with a Royal Marines helmet plate attached to the front. He is equipped with pattern 1908 webbing and his bayonet scabbard is made of brown leather, the order to blacken them not yet having been issued.

Above right: Around his ankles, this Marine wears webbing leggings with leather closure tabs, a pattern introduced before the First World War and still in service at this time. His webbing set is minimal and neither haversack nor water bottle carrier is fitted. The epaulettes at the shoulders are buttoned over the braces of his equipment to prevent them from slipping off of his shoulders during movement.

 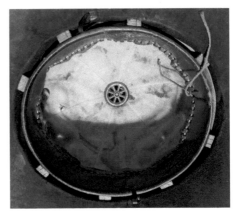

The Royal Marines wore a distinctive Wolseley pattern helmet in tropical stations during the interwar period. This cork helmet has a simple band, rather than a folded puggaree, and has been whitened with blanco. A Royal Marine helmet plate has been fitted to the front of the helmet and has the Latin motto of the force: 'Per Mare, Per Terram', or 'By Sea, By Land'. Note the early style sweat band, which is sewn to cork blocks and not removable on this helmet.

The sailors landed from these ships were dressed in the traditional white naval cotton-duck uniforms of the period and were equipped with the navy's own style of sun helmet. Naval landing parties were lightly armed with Enfield rifles and Lewis light machine guns, but when supported by the guns of a cruiser acting as a floating gun battery, the sailors were a potent force. Thankfully, they were never required to go into battle, though it had been a close run thing.

Palestine

In order to secure support for the First World War in the Middle East, Britain and her allies had made a number of promises to different local players that offered concessions to them in peacetime in exchange for support against the Ottomans. Two of these promises were incompatible with each other and would sow the seeds for a discord that has lasted to the present day.

The secret Sykes-Picot agreement in 1916 had carved up post-war influence in the region, with Britain having control of the area between the coast and the River Jordan, along with Jordan and southern Iraq, while France would exert influence over Syria, northern Iraq and Lebanon. Alongside this secret agreement was a series of letters sent between the British High Commissioner of Egypt and the Sharif of Mecca, Hussein bin Ali. These letters indicated that the British would recognise Arab independence in the region in exchange for help against the Ottoman Empire. Whether this was truly a treaty or not is open to debate; however, the Arabs certainly felt it constituted one and launched the Arab Revolt in fulfilment of their part of the agreement. The third agreement made in 1917 during the First World War was the Balfour Declaration that committed the British Government to supporting the establishment of a Jewish homeland in Palestine.

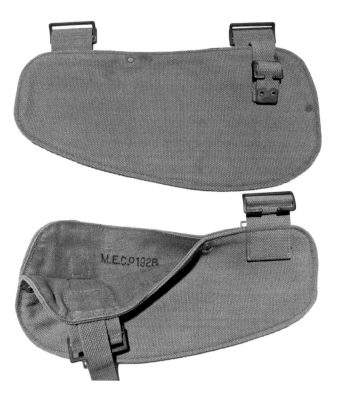

Although the Army had dropped the entrenching tool and its carrier in 1923, the Royal Navy continued to use the tool and limited numbers of the kidney-shaped carrier continued to be manufactured. The cover was used not only for storing the metal entrenching tool head, but also small items such as shoe polish, dubbin and the rifle pull through. This example was manufactured by the Mills Equipment Company in 1928 and a very faint 'N' stamp can be seen across from the date stamp.

Although declared obsolete by the Army on 6 September 1923, the entrenching tool remained in service with the Royal Navy throughout the interwar period. The design was based on an Indian Army pattern known as the Sirhind tool and featured a pointed spade on one end and a pick on the other. The tool broke down into two pieces, a cast iron head and the wooden helve made of ash or hickory.

This alternative method of securing the pattern 1908 waist belt became popular in the interwar period. This method was trickier to assemble and more difficult to undo in a hurry than that used previously, but looked smarter as the loose end of the belt was tucked out of sight.

These agreements were clearly incompatible and the League of Nations, established in the wake of the First World War, had the difficult job of finding some sort of solution. The League of Nations decided to make Palestine a Class A Mandate under British control. This meant the region was to be administered by the British for the foreseeable future, until 'such time as [it was] able to stand on its own'. Throughout the 1920s and 1930s, the British oversaw a delicate peace between the Palestinians, Arabs and Jewish settlers. Although outright warfare was avoided, rioting, acts of terrorism and civil unrest were endemic in the region.

Things had started off peaceably enough in the 1920s, with only minor grumbles and the occasional riot. However, increasing tensions brought about by growing Jewish immigration came to a head in 1929 when the High Commissioner was on leave. A large-scale Jewish demonstration took place in Tel Aviv with the shouting of Zionist slogans and the waving of Jewish flags. This was countered by local Muslims descending on the Western or 'Wailing' Wall in Jerusalem and destroying Jewish holy books and prayers. Within a week, large-scale rioting had broken out among the Arab population of Jerusalem and violence quickly spread outside the city. The British had only 292 reliable British policemen available to them, the locally recruited Jewish and Arab police being seen as too compromised to be trusted in the powder keg that was coming close to blowing. British police and troops were rapidly drafted in from nearby Egypt, but by the end of the crisis 133 Jews had been killed with 339 wounded and 116 Arabs were dead with a further 232 wounded. It was clear that the British had too few trustworthy police or soldiers in the region to deal with inter-religious violence and the following decade saw a rise in the numbers of British military personnel deployed to the Mandate. The violence continued despite the increase in military and by 1936 there was an Arab rebellion that manifested itself as violence against Jewish settlers, the British and other Arab groups as different factions fought for weapons, funds and supporters. More troops continued to be brought into Palestine, including artillery, engineers and armoured cars, although morale among the British Army was low, one officer remarking, 'the soldiers hate the whole thing and would prefer martial law.'

Martial law, however, was something the British could not impose at this stage, for fear of inciting the local citizenry against them even more. British troops were instead deployed in defensive postures, guarding key points that allowed the roads and railways to remain open. The military continued to press the civil authorities for more freedom to respond robustly to threats, while the Colonial Office wanted more restraint and efforts put into reconciliation between the Arabs and Jews. This was not to be the case, however, and 1937 saw increasing violence from Arab groups and a more robust response from the British military and police with laws banning the private ownership of firearms together with heavy fines for those harbouring suspected insurgents. One British woman wrote, 'a terrific battle is in progress all-round the Safed hills, the aeroplanes have been passing backwards and forwards all day from Samakh.'

Life for the average British soldier during this period was a mixture of fear and boredom. With little to do and insufficient funds, some found a less than legal way of supplementing their pay by selling everything that wasn't nailed down!

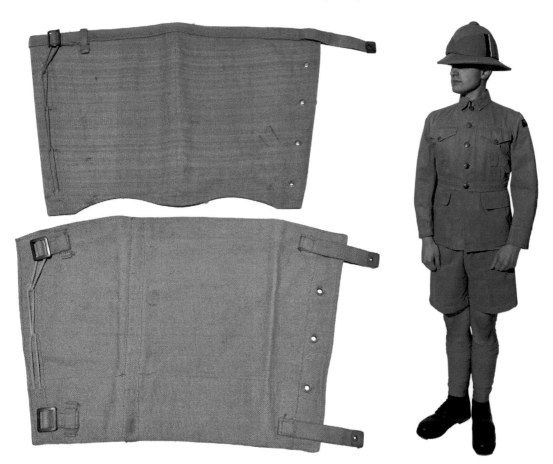

Above left: The Royal Navy issued its men leggings produced of pre-shrunk cotton webbing to protect the bottoms of sailors' trouser legs when operating away from their ship. 'Mills Naval Pattern Leggings' (*lower*) were adopted by the Royal Navy shortly after the pattern 1919, though they are not part of that equipment set. This design was the most common pattern through the 1920s and had two webbing tabs, at the top and bottom, with three sets of loops and eyelets between. In the 1930s this pattern was updated, with the lower webbing tab removed and replaced with a fourth loop and eyelet (*upper*).

Above right: The RAF helped police many parts of the Empire in the interwar period and in Iraq the RAF commanded an inter-service unit formed in 1922 and initially based in Baghdad. By 1928, however, the headquarters were at RAF Hinaidi, just outside the city. This smartly turned out airman is based at this station and is dressed ready for parade. He wears an early pattern of RAF khaki drill tunic which is closely based on the blue serge Service Dress uniform with a stand and fall collar secured by three brass hooks, five button closure, breast pockets with pointed flaps, integral belt, concealed skirt pockets and plain cuffs. As an airman, he has embroidered eagles sewn to the top of each sleeve at the shoulder and an RAF flash on the puggaree of his sun helmet.

The pattern 1925 web equipment set was adopted by the Royal Air Force in 1927 and was manufactured in blue-grey for them. Both rifle and pistol sets were acquired, but both configurations shared the same belt, shoulder braces, rucksack and haversack. The rucksack comprised an upper and lower portion and had straps on the outside that allowed a helmet to be secured. The water bottle was carried in a sleeve-type webbing carrier attached to the ends of the shoulder braces and the haversack was similar to that used in the 1919 pattern, but without the separate straps on the base. During the interwar years, the RAF reserved pattern 1925 for Home Service, while pattern 1908 continued to be issued for service overseas.

We were all hard up, while I was in debt... we conceived all sorts of schemes. On pay day "Friday" all the boys in our hut would toss their wages onto one bed and pool the lot, a trustworthy treasurer being appointed to supply cigarettes, beer, etc., rationing them for one week. Everything that could be taken out of the camp was sold to some Jewish dealer in Jaffa Road, Haifa – fire extinguishers, picks & shovels and even some spare wheels. The convoys on the road coasted down every hill with their engines switched off to save petrol, most of the big lorries did an average of ten miles to a gallon, so quite a lot of petrol was saved and sold for ten piasters per gallon (two bob). On one occasion a couple of donkeys disappeared, sold I believe, to an Arab in the village of Samak. The Quartermaster's stores lost hundreds of blankets and other equipment, in fact Jaffa Road was like Paddy's Market, Liverpool on a Saturday afternoon, we could flog anything...

The British troops in Palestine were used for general peacekeeping that differed significantly from others parts of the Empire. These duties included the potentially dangerous business of stopping suspicious looking civilians, either Jewish or Arab, and searching them for illegal weapons. As the penalty for possession of illegal weapons was death, those that were carrying them often decided that they had nothing to lose and would respond with violence.

Other duties included regular patrols to ensure the highways were kept clear. The majority of vehicles travelling up and down Palestine belonged to the British, but these were limited to the metalled roads; for patrols further afield horses, and even camels, were used to give men the necessary mobility. These patrols were on the look-out for Arab and Jewish armed groups as well as deserters and those involved in criminal activities; in Palestine the distinction between soldier and policeman was a fluid one.

The most obvious cross-over between the two forces was in the quelling of riots, where police and the army worked directly alongside one another. Most of the time riots could be dealt with by men armed with shields and pickaxe handles, but occasionally lethal force was employed if a mob became too out of hand. There were repeated claims of police and army brutality against the local population, although, as one officer pointed out,

> At times tempers flared, soldiers would see Arab atrocities and there were some of their mates killed and on occasions, they, the troops became bloody angry. In the heat of an action, when a prisoner is brought in, you see your friend near you – you think "shoot the b...d" and I know of one or two occasions when this happened. But it is a source of great pride to all, as a British soldier, that you can count such incidents on the fingers of one hand…

Ditty boxes were used until 1937 by sailors to hold their precious personal belongings. They were one of the few places a sailor could keep items securely on ship, a lock being fitted to the lid. They were used to hold photographs, letters and valuable personal belongings. The sailor's name was marked on the front with a brass plaque and the original owner of this box has decorated it with a painted Union flag on the lid.

This cover of *The War Illustrated* from October 1918 shows a British sentry on guard at the Gate of Damascus. His kit consists of a Wolseley pattern helmet, collarless shirt, shorts, hose tops, puttees, pattern 1908 webbing and an SMLE rifle with bayonet. This uniform was the mainstay of British soldiers serving in the Middle East in the 1920s and 1930s and was largely unchanged right up until the Second World War.

The British soldier in Palestine was equipped much the same as anywhere else in the Empire, with khaki drill uniform, 1908 pattern webbing and a Short Magazine Lee-Enfield (SMLE) rifle. The wearing of steel helmets was more common in Palestine than elsewhere because of the risk of rioting, the bowl-shaped steel helmet being just as effective at protecting from bricks as it was from shrapnel. The nature of the work in Palestine also influenced a more casual approach to dress codes, much as life on the North West Frontier of India had done. The cool temperatures on an evening meant that it was not uncommon for men to wear a woollen cardigan or jumper over their khaki drill uniform. It was also common to combine the woollen service dress uniform jacket with shorts to meet the needs of the climate.

1938 finally brought the Army the freedom of operations they so desperately craved and the end of the Munich Crisis prompted an increase in troop numbers in the Mandate, rising to 20,000 by the end of the year. The charismatic Colonel Orde Wingate also found an outlet for his unique talents at this point, creating 'Special Night Squads' of British troops and Jewish irregulars to combat the Arab revolt by marching long distances at night to strike guerrillas in their villages before slipping away again. 1938 also saw a systematic village-by-village search for illegal firearms and harsh punishments for both individuals and communities that harboured them, which saw Arab resistance almost completely quashed by 1939.

Above left: The British Army helped maintain an uneasy peace in Palestine between the two world wars. This soldier is stationed in the Mandate and is sounding his bugle at dawn to awaken his comrades for the day ahead. He wears a First World War vintage 'helmet, steel, Mark I' and has an early style of khaki drill shirt with buttons to secure the collar open, short sleeves and no epaulettes. He holds his rifle by his side to make it easier to use his bugle and he wears tall puttees with hose tops. Around his waist is tied a cotton bandolier with fifty rounds of .303 ammunition.

Above right: From the rear, it can be seen that the bugle is carried on a long coloured cord. The length of this cord provides enough slack to allow it to be brought up to the mouth to be blown, without having to be unslung. It can be seen that this soldier has tucked the chin strap for his helmet to the rear. This was a common way of wearing the steel helmet when it was unlikely that the wearer would be going into action, being more comfortable to wear for long periods and easier to remove or replace the helmet. In a combat situation, however, the helmet could be easily dislodged and fall off, so this method of wear was discouraged.

Above left: This sapper from the Royal Engineers is keeping guard for a work detail in Palestine in the late 1930s. The threat of attack from either Jewish or Arab independence movements was still relatively low, but remained a worry to the British authorities in the Mandate and so precautions were taken, including posting sentries for work parties. The sentry wears a woollen collarless shirt in a khaki green colour. This pattern was starting to replace the old 'greyback' design that had seen service since the Victorian era, the darker colour offering a greater level of camouflage when men were in shirt sleeve order. He wears this with a pair of khaki drill shorts and a pair of short puttees. The service dress cap bears the badge of his corps, the sovereign's cypher inside a laurel wreath.

Above right: As he is part of a work detail, this soldier wears his webbing in Fatigue Order with only water bottle and haversack, each slung across the chest on a shoulder brace. This was a minimal set of webbing designed to give a soldier a way to carry food and water for the day when he was unlikely to need ammunition. The two components could be easily taken off while the soldier worked, but a soldierly appearance was retained during the march to and from the work site. This sentry would have the ten rounds in the internal magazine of his SMLE, but no further ammunition.

Webbing was cleaned and coloured using a powder called blanco, manufactured by Pickerings. This powder was pressed into solid cakes and, when wetted, made up a paste that could be applied over the cotton webbing with a brush or a piece of sponge. The blanco was messy and easily broken, so special tins were available that protected the fragile block and prevented it from staining other items in a man's kitbag.

First field dressings were carried by each individual soldier, often in an internal skirt pocket of the service dress jacket. Each cloth pack contained two dressings, for entry and exit wounds. This example was made by Arthur Berton Ltd in 1929. Shell dressings were larger than first field dressings and consisted of a large, sterilised, absorbent pad that could be placed over a wound and then secured to apply pressure. First World War shell dressings continued to be used throughout the interwar period as there were great numbers left in store after the war. The First World War examples shown here include a small vial of iodine to help sterilise the wound before the dressing is applied. Instructions for field and shell dressing use are printed on the outer cloth packaging.

This surge of troops in 1938 saw some of the first combat use of the new 1937 pattern webbing equipment as it was sent out with some of the reinforcing units. This new webbing system, along with the soon to be famous Bren gun, was rolled out to several units that were rotated out to the Mandate and some of the earliest photographs of its use depict soldiers from the King's Own Regiment in Palestine in 1938.

Palestine was not an easy posting for British soldiers and would remain an unpopular destination throughout the war until the British pulled out in 1948 as the state of Israel came into being. The interwar period saw a rising tide of violence in the Mandate and the intransigence of all three parties and the conflicting promises made twenty years earlier ensured there would not be a peaceable solution in the short term.

The Mark IV service respirator was introduced in 1926 and was a major advance over the earlier Mk III model. The mask used a separate filter box that drew in contaminated air and scrubbed it of gas particulates. The air was drawn up the hose to the face piece and the dry air was directed over the eye pieces to reduce the effect of condensation. The face piece was made of moulded rubber, with a large round metal exhale valve on the front. Early masks were made of orange rubber covered in a tan stockinet that helped protect it from abrasions and damage. This mask is dated 1936 with a 1939-dated Filter Type E Mk V painted tan. These filters used blue asbestos pads and activated charcoal to remove gas from the air.

The first Mk IV respirators had No. 4 Mk I head harnesses, consisting of a diamond-shaped piece of tan canvas with adjustable elastic straps sewn to the corners, connecting with the six buckles on the face piece. This example is prominently marked with the date, 1929, and the War Department Broad Arrow.

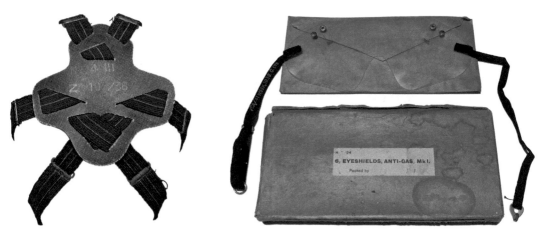

Above left: A new rubber head harness, the No. 4 Mk III, was introduced to give the masks greater stability when worn. These were made in black, with dates of manufacture stamped in white ink, like the October 1936 date seen on this example. Each elastic strap was fully adjustable with metal tensioning buckles.

Above right: Celluloid eye shields were supplied in the late interwar years as part of the anti-gas equipment to protect a soldier's eyes from droplets of irritant gas. Each was made of a simple stamped piece of clear or yellowed plastic, with press studs that were used to provide a small modicum of shape to the eye shield. Elastic tapes held the eye shield onto the soldier's head and each pair was packaged in an individual paper envelope. These envelopes were provided in sets of six in a rectangular cardboard box. A paper label gave information on the contents and had space to stamp the date of production, in this case 1938.

To prevent condensation build-up on the lenses of respirators, anti-dimming outfits were issued. These contained a cloth at one end of a metal tube and a paste made of Red Turkey Oil, a sulphonated castor oil, at the other; the cloth was used to spread the paste on the inside of the respirator lens. This Mk V tin was produced in 1935 and has instructions for its use printed on the outside of the cylinder.

PLAYER'S CIGARETTES

TRANS-JORDAN FRONTIER FORCE

Left: The Transjordan Frontier Force was formed in 1926 to replace a British gendarmerie in the British Mandate. The force consisted of British officers and senior NCOs and locally recruited other ranks. For the period and region, the force was ethnically diverse. While Palestinian Arabs made up the bulk of the unit, Jews, Arabs and Circassians made up to a quarter of the force. This sergeant wears typical garb; his uniform is the traditional khaki drill but he has blue puttees and a red cummerbund indicating his status as a sergeant. On his head he wears a traditional kalpak, an Ottoman headdress made of wool, with the badge of the Frontier Force mounted centrally.

Below: This cotton bandolier saw extensive use in the interwar period. The original date of manufacture was 1918 and this can be seen on the left; it was then refilled and reissued by the Royal Navy in 1929 and 1939. The details of the reloads were stamped onto the fabric in green ink. This bandolier is the Mk II design that was introduced into service in 1906. Each pocket was initially secured with either snap fasteners or buttons, but bent-over copper wire hooks were introduced in 1916. The stampings on the bandolier indicate that it held fifty rounds of Mk VII .303 ammunition. Note the 'N' stamp for Royal Navy ownership included on each reload stamp. The older filling markings on the left have been cancelled by a large green cross.

6

The Rest of Empire

For the military across the Empire, the interwar period was one of contraction, cost cutting and soul searching as countries tried to reconcile anti-war feelings in the populace with the growing menace of another looming conflict. The First World War had seen massive expansions in the armed forces of Canada, Australia and South Africa, and on the back of their sacrifices these nations were flexing their independence from Great Britain, especially in areas of defence, foreign policy and internal affairs. Britain maintained close links with all her dominions, but she could no longer be sure of a blank cheque in time of conflict.

For Canada and Australia, the interwar period was relatively stable, with little external threat and a consequent neglect of the national military and militias. For South Africa, there were continuing tensions with indigenous tribesmen and the roles of the army and police became ever more intertwined. Ironically, these much smaller militaries could afford to innovate in the late 1920s and into the 1930s. The British Army was so large that the cost of new equipment was prohibitively expensive, while the smaller partners in the Empire, with their much more modest armed forces, were able to experiment with new designs of accoutrements and personal and field kit. These trials of equipment gave each nation's infantry a distinctive look in the late interwar period and some of the ideas introduced would be adopted by Great Britain in the Second World War. Others would sadly fizzle out without adoption except for this brief window in peacetime.

Canada

Following the demobilisation of the Canadian Expeditionary Force in 1918, a committee chaired by General Otter considered what form Canada's peacetime armed forces should take. It was agreed that the country should field four cavalry and eleven infantry divisions with the requisite support troops for a force of this size. In total, this would have given an establishment of 300,000 men. This was clearly a complete fantasy, as there would never be the requisite number of men or resources to equip them. By 1922–23, only 38,000 of the required 130,000 Militia actually took part in annual training. One area in which the Otter Committee did achieve success was in reforming the structure of Canada's armed forces to draw on the traditions of both the militia and the Canadian Expeditionary Force. The old numbered titles for most regiments were dropped and replaced with titles that reflected a regiment's heritage and area of recruiting. The large single Canadian infantry regiment was replaced by three units, including one drawn heavily from the French Canadian population to try and better integrate this segment of the population into the armed forces.

Canada effectively abandoned a regular armed force in the interwar period, instead looking to the part-time militia to fill the gap. The professional full-time soldiers of the First World War gradually retired and the Canadian army lost much of its hard-won expertise. This was coupled with minuscule defence budgets and a wider antipathy to the armed forces following the First World War. Equipment was not replaced and gradually became obsolescent, as did the army's doctrine. The only way Canadian officers could get any staff experience was to travel across the Atlantic to Great Britain to the staff colleges there. The Great Depression hit Canada hard and the funding for the militia fell to just $1.9 million in 1931–32, down from $11 million a year in 1922–23. Following the Chanak Crisis, Canada took on an increasingly neutral and isolationist stance, desperately trying to avoid being drawn into overseas conflicts. Accordingly, a law was passed in 1937 making it illegal for Canadians to enlist to fight in other countries' wars. This law was widely ignored and Canadians went overseas to support the Republican forces in the Spanish Civil War.

Between the wars, Canada maintained a small permanent military force, supplemented by a part-time militia. Chronically underfunded, decisions had to be made as to where to allocate funds during the interwar period. As such, Canada issued cotton drill uniforms for wear in the hot summer months to its Permanent Force, while the Non-Permanent Militia had to swelter in their woollen service dress. This Regular of the Royal Canadian Regiment wears the Canadian Pattern of the 'Other Ranks' khaki drill service dress jacket. This pattern was made in a distinctive light green shade and could be worn with either shorts or trousers. Additionally, these jackets were secured with five removable large brass buttons and featured a stand and fall collar, pointed pocket flaps, brass belt hooks, patrol pattern back and pointed cuffs. This man's webbing is the pattern 1925 set from the Mills Equipment Company in Great Britain, confusingly known in Canada as pattern 1919. On his head he wears the woollen service dress cap, with brown leather chin strap and a brass cap badge secured to the front. Typically for a Canadian regiment, he wears his tall puttees without hose tops and is armed with the standard SMLE rifle.

Above left: From the rear, details of the pattern 1925 set can be seen, including the narrower braces with wider shoulder flares, an internal loop on the left brace to help keep the pair together, a bayonet frog with press stud attachment to the belt and a water bottle carrier made of 1-inch webbing.

Above right: The Mills Equipment Company continued developing new designs in the interwar years, though buyers were scarce with large stockpiles of spare equipment. The pattern 1925 web equipment set was purchased in small amounts by South Africa and Canada, with the latter referring to it as pattern 1919. The new design was lightened, reducing the ammunition capacity from 150 rounds in the 1908 pattern to 120 rounds, with four pockets per cartridge carrier. Like the Naval pattern 1919 set, it had narrower shoulder braces and utilised an adjustable back strap, which was connected directly to the integral cartridge carriers. A haversack and water bottle in its carrier hung down below the belt. This pattern was not produced in large numbers, nor did it entirely supplant the 1908 pattern in either country.

The stiff pre-First World War service dress cap was reintroduced after the end of the conflict, slightly recut to provide the smarter appearance demanded of the post-war peacetime army. This cap conforms to the revised pattern sealed in 1921 and has a larger peak than the earlier pattern as well as a top stitch on the top of the head band.

One area of definite growth between the wars was the Canadian Navy, which went through a massive expansion in 1920, when the nation was offered a cruiser and two destroyers by Great Britain. This formed the nucleus of the interwar Royal Canadian Navy and was based in Halifax, supported by a small fleet of trawlers that were used as minesweepers. The small fleet was mainly used to patrol territorial waters and enforce fishing regulations, the voyages doubling up as opportunities to train personnel. The first significant contribution made by the RCN was in 1932, when open revolt broke out in El Salvador. The British Consul was concerned for British and Empire subjects living in the troubled country and their property. It was impractical to send a warship from the Royal Navy, so the RCN was asked to intervene. The RCN destroyer *Skeena* was dispatched to the country and five British women who were concerned for their safety were taken aboard while the captain and his executive officer went ashore to reconnoitre the port of Acajutla. The Salvadorian military restored order the following month, executing 20,000 of its own people in the process. The Royal Canadian Navy, however, had proven its utility in responding to international situations in the Western Hemisphere, out of reach of the Royal Navy.

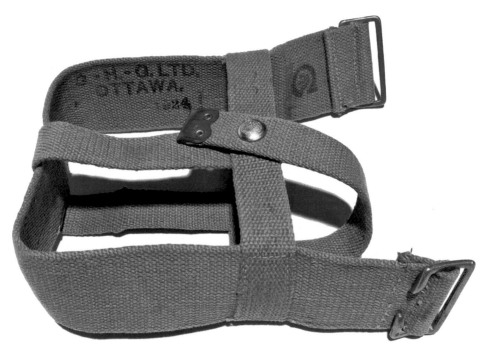

Despite looking for a new webbing set to replace the 1908 system, Canada retained large quantities of the older design until the outbreak of the Second World War. These were issued to the militia and held as a strategic reserve, should the country need to rapidly mobilise her forces. Small quantities of new components were manufactured to maintain this stockpile, such as this water bottle carrier, manufactured by Grant-Holden-Graham Ltd of Ottawa in 1924. The large Broad Arrow within a 'C' stamp indicates Canadian military ownership. The design is identical to those manufactured during the First World War, with a front-mounted press stud to hold the securing strap, rather than the top-mounted version introduced into British Army service in 1921.

In line with the rest of the Empire, the late 1930s saw a change of policy with the threat of war due to the rise to power of Hitler in Germany. The Canadian Defence Minister Mackenzie King gave his assurance to Great Britain that if war were to be declared, Canada would support Britain. This led to a growth in military spending and recruitment in the last two years of peace and the development of indigenous manufacturers of military arms and accoutrements. In 1938, a crucial step towards modernisation took place when the first orders were placed for the new Bren gun to replace the venerable Lewis gun, while the Canadian Armoured Fighting Vehicles School was established in Ottawa in the same year. The interwar period saw Canada's armed forces dwindle to a moribund force; underfunded and with poor morale. Yet the looming war clouds in Europe, as elsewhere, jolted the Canucks out of their complacency and major investments in the military in 1938 and early 1939 ensured that there was a nucleus around which the forces needed for war could be built.

In 1926 it became official policy for soldiers to blacken and treat the leather part of the bayonet scabbard with paraffin wax. Manufacturers were also instructed to produce scabbards in waxed black leather, rather than brown. These treated scabbards were marked with a 'W' on the back of the leather near the seam. The No. 1 Mk II scabbards shown above were manufactured in the First World War, with the left scabbard in the earlier brown finish and the right scabbard treated and blackened after the First World War.

This pair of pattern 1907 sword bayonets illustrate the refurbishment programme introduced in the 1920s. The example on the left has been refinished, as evidenced by the added 1924 date and the original bluing on the lower portion of the ricasso. The example on the right has been left in its original finish and has escaped the refurbishment programme.

Australia

Like much of the rest of the Empire, Australia had relied on a part-time militia before the First World War. During the First World War, the country had raised an imperial expeditionary force which had won great renown for the newly formed nation. In the aftermath of the conflict, however, the Australian Imperial Force (AIF) was disbanded and the country reverted to its pre-war militia. The overall title for Australia's army between the wars was the 'Australian Military Force', which in turn was made up of a small full-time professional force known as the 'Permanent Military Force' and a part-time militia known as the 'Citizen Military Force'. This structure had been agreed on in 1920, when the AIF was stood down, with the plan that Australia would need to deploy 270,000 men if another conflict were to take place and a peacetime force maintained of approximately half that strength through compulsory enlistment. There was no appetite for conscription among the war-weary Australian populace and the force dwindled from 127,000 in 1921 to just 37,000 in 1922. In 1929, the new Labour government removed the compulsory element from the force and reinstated the title of militia to highlight that it was to henceforth be an all-volunteer force. The only thing this change succeeded in doing was dropping the number of men in Australia's armed forces even further, and despite promises of new equipment and weapons, the force continued to soldier on with First World War surplus right up until the Second World War.

As elsewhere in the Empire, funding was severely limited throughout the interwar period and it was not until 1935 that more money began to be allocated to the militia. Funding increased in 1937, as war clouds loomed, with the aim of doubling the size of the Australian militia. A recruiting drive in 1938 saw 8,000 men join in just three months, increasing the size of the military to 43,000. By 1939, it had risen further to over 80,000 volunteers serving on a part-time basis, though there was a massive shortage of equipment and weapons, which left the Australian Army far from prepared when war broke out in 1939.

The Australian military had a fairly peaceable interlude between the two world wars. However, in 1927, HMAS *Adelaide* was sent on a punitive expedition to the island of Malaita in the British Solomon Islands. Kwaio natives had murdered a district officer and sixteen others, so the ship deployed three platoons to search for the perpetrators. This force was mainly made up of civilians armed with rifles and bent on revenge, although fifty men from the *Adelaide* were added to try and hold the armed party in check. The civilian volunteers quickly became a liability, as they had been led to believe they would be allowed to shoot the natives on sight and were most upset to find that this was not the case. They were also heavy drinkers and gamblers and found the terrain too difficult to traverse, so most were dismissed within two weeks. The naval personnel suffered from malaria and dysentery: indeed, when HMAS *Adelaide* returned to Sydney a fifth of the crew needed to be hospitalised with tropical diseases. The rebellion was swiftly and brutally put down by the local police forces, desirous of revenge for their murdered colleagues, and the number of native dead is

Above left: Despite its proud service during the First World War, Australia's military was in a parlous state between the two world wars. The full-time AIF was disbanded and a part-time militia reinstated. This militiaman has joined as part of the recruitment drive of the late 1930s and stands newly equipped and ready for his annual camp. He wears the fifty-round leather bandolier and waist belt from the pattern 1903 set as well as a 'carrier, water bottle, O.S.' and a 'haversack, other services'. He wears the distinctive Australian slouch hat, but with its brim turned down to protect him from the sun. A red stripe in his hat's puggaree indicates his status as a member of the militia and he wears the issue brown boots with a pair of Australian-made three-button woollen gaiters. His service dress tunic is also made locally and fastened up the front with darkened metal buttons.

Above right: The rear of this militiaman shows the number of straps required for the different components of his load-bearing equipment. The 12-inch sword bayonet rests over his left hip in a pattern 1914 bayonet frog, as no frog was originally included in the pattern 1903 bandolier equipment set. The Short Magazine Lee-Enfield No. 1 Mk III rifle was standard issue across the Empire and Australia had its own arms factory at Lithgow, which had been in operation since 1912, producing both SMLEs and their requisite bayonets.

estimated between fifty and 200. The Australian presence was probably unnecessary but was appreciated as a sign of solidarity between the Government of Australia and its British-controlled neighbours.

Above left: Every soldier was equipped with an enamelled mug. Between the wars, these were usually white with blue rims and handles and were often seen attached to the back of a webbing pack. The blue enamel was harder wearing than white, but more expensive to manufacture and so was only used on areas likely to chip easily, like the rim.

Above right: Rum was issued to men at the discretion of an officer. It was used to help ward off cold at night and to offer a small amount of 'Dutch courage' before men went into action. Rum, along with other liquid stores, was supplied in glazed earthenware jars that came in ½, 1 and 2 gallon sizes. The letters 'SRD' indicated military ownership and stood for the 'Supply Reserve Depot', although the men often joked that it actually stood for 'seldom reaches destination' or 'soon runs dry'.

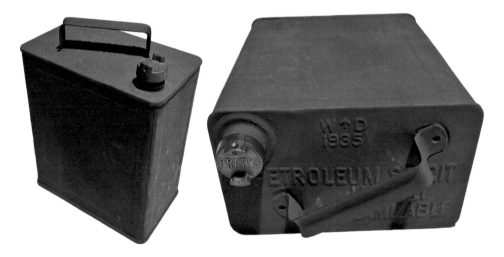

Standard 1-gallon fuel cans were in widespread use by both civilians and the military between the wars. They were flimsy and frequently leaked, but were used for transporting not only fuel but also water and other liquids. This example has the Broad Arrow indicating military ownership and the date of 1935 pressed into the metal on the top of the can. As these cans were often used to carry petrol, a warning is also included indicating the potentially flammable nature of the contents.

Binoculars between the wars were almost exclusively of the prismatic type, as these lenses gave better magnification and a clearer sight picture than the earlier galvanic type of lenses. A number of different patterns were in use which, despite differing in details, were broadly similar. On the left is a 1918-dated pair of No. 3 Mk II binoculars and on the right is a 1939-dated pair of No. 2 Mk II binoculars. Both have the Broad Arrow mark of War Department ownership stamped into the front face. A textured coating is applied to the lens barrels to aid grip and loops are provided to allow them to be slung by a strap around the neck.

South Africa

The Union of South Africa's military was the Union Defence Force (UDF), which had been formed in 1912. The law that created this new force had also obliged all white males between the ages of seventeen and sixty to serve; this was unnecessary, however, as the popularity of the service early on ensured ample volunteers. The UDF served well during the First World War, both in Africa against German colonies and in Europe on the Western Front. The military was segregated from the start, but 146,000 white and 83,000 black men served during the First World War, taking 18,600 casualties, of whom 12,452 were killed.

Immediately following the First World War, the South African military was restructured, with an air force formed in 1920 and a naval service in 1922. 1922 also saw the Permanent Force reorganised with a greater emphasis on staff and support corps than had previously been the case. The Permanent Force was made up of long-serving career soldiers, who were supported by the Active Citizen Force, made up of temporary conscripts fulfilling their obligations to the state. Like so many nations, the Great Depression hit the South African military hard and to save money a number of units in the Permanent Force were disbanded, as were fifty-six Citizen Force units. The Naval Service, founded just a few years before, was abolished in 1934 because the shortage of funding was so great. Happily, a change of policy was enacted by the new Minister of Defence, Oswald Pirow, in 1935 that saw expenditure on the military increased, with the aim of increasing the size of the Permanent Force and Active Citizen Force to 56,000 men with a reserve of 100,000. By 1936, major expansion of the Army and the South African Air Force had taken place and the following year, the Minister of Defence informed the country that he intended to expand the UDF further with a

Above left: Set up in 1914, the Somaliland Camel Corps was tasked with defending this British protectorate during the interwar period. Like most colonial forces in Africa, it was officered by the British and its askari were recruited locally in Somalia. The uniform adopted by the corps was distinctive, with men wearing a woollen pullover with khaki drill patches on the shoulders. They wore boots, bare feet or, in this case, chaplis leather sandals on their feet. Above these, a pair of blue puttees was worn. Across the shoulder was a leather pattern 1903 bandolier and the headgear consisted of a kullah with a puggaree wrapped around, the tail of which was worn loose down the back. This sergeant displays his rank with yellow embroidered badges on the sleeves of his jumper and a red sash worn across the body.

Above right: This native sergeant-major belongs to the Gold Coast Regiment, part of the Royal West African Frontier Force which recruited in what is today Ghana. This regiment was officered by the British, but the men and NCOs were drawn from the local populations. This soldier wears the parade dress of the regiment, which was a simple modification of the usual khaki drill field uniform. Over the shirt is worn an elaborate red and gold waistcoat, while a red cummerbund is worn around the waist of the shorts. A leather sword belt is buckled over this and he wears a traditional fez with a gilded cap badge.

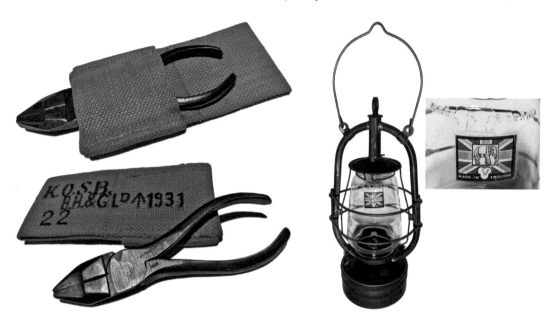

Above left: Pliers were essential tools for repairing weapons, communications equipment and wires. This pair of 1918-dated side-cutting pliers is carried in a 1931-dated webbing frog from the rare 'Web Equipment, Royal Artillery' set. This was a specialised set of accoutrements developed for use by the artillery in the interwar period. It was only produced in small numbers and would become obsolete during the Second World War, as the Army adopted the pattern 1937 set for all its branches. The pliers frog survived the rest of the set's obsolescence, however, and continued to be manufactured long after the Second World War. This frog was made by Barrow, Hepburn & Gale Ltd.

Above right: Paraffin-fuelled hurricane lamps were essential for lighting in many parts of the Empire where electric lighting had yet to be installed. This lamp, manufactured by Veritas Pax, is typical of these simple forms of illumination. They were essential tools for British soldiers as they allowed field camps to be lit at night and provided illumination when inspecting unlit native dwellings for suspected insurgents.

plan to put £5 million in place over the coming three years. The outbreak of the Second World War would, of course, change these plans, but the UDF and SAAF were in a far healthier position in 1939 than they had been just five years earlier.

Part of the reorganisation and improvement of the UDF involved upgrading the accoutrements and personal equipment of the Force's infantry. South Africa had purchased 1908, 1913 and 1925 pattern web equipment in the past and in 1934 the Mills Equipment Co. Ltd of London was contracted to supply a new webbing set. Mills had been trying to persuade the British Government to purchase its new Braithwaite Committee design of web equipment without much success, so when the South African Government approached them the new design was offered up and it is believed the Union ordered several thousand sets, which were manufactured by 1936. There was never enough of the equipment to issue the new pattern to the entire UDF, so it was prioritised to certain units such as the Special Service Battalion, Transvaal Scottish and possibly others as well.

Above left: The South African infantry of the late 1930s had developed its own distinct uniform, quite different from any other part of the Empire. For the Permanent Force, the large Wolseley and solar pith helmets used elsewhere were replaced with a much smaller design, known as a 'polo' helmet. The webbing was the commercially produced Braithwaite pattern that was introduced in the mid-1930s. Funds were never sufficient to allow this new pattern to be rolled out to all of South Africa's armed forces, so it was used alongside the older pattern 1908 and pattern 1903 equipment sets.

Above right: This private of the Kimberley Regiment stands easy at the start of a drill session in 1938. He wears khaki drill shorts and jacket. The Union Defence Force issued its men with brown leather ankle boots and three and four-strap webbing leggings replaced tall puttees in the 1930s, which secured up the front with webbing tapes and matching brass buckles. It is apparent that the shoulder braces on the Braithwaite pattern equipment are the thinner type used on the pattern 1919 and 1925 sets, rather than the 2-inch-wide braces of the older 1908 pattern. The three-piece belt is also evident here, which was a common feature to the most of interwar webbing designs.

In keeping with the trend of interwar webbing designs, this new pattern was designed for mobility and was much lighter than the earlier 1908 pattern. The number of pockets on cartridge carriers continued to be reduced with ten pockets on the 1908 pattern, eight pockets on the 1925 pattern and just six pockets on this new design. The biggest change was in the design of the pack, which was based on the 1925 pattern design, but with differing proportions for the two parts of the rucksack, the most distinctive feature being straps on the rear to accommodate a short shovel or pick. Alongside this new web equipment, the UDF became one of the first forces in the Empire to adopt aluminium rectangular mess tins that were both lighter and more hygienic than the earlier tinned iron patterns.

The South African UDF had a unique style of sun helmet known as a 'polo' helmet. This design had been adopted in 1930, tested in 1932 and issued out to troops in 1934. These helmets were produced in South Africa by South African Pith Helmet Industries and were made of compressed cork. The helmet was considered better suited for bush warfare in Africa than the earlier Wolseley design, with initial field testing occurring during the Ipumbu Uprising in 1932.

South Africa had a complex system of puggaree flashes in use during both the interwar period and the early years of the Second World War. Each regiment was assigned a unique design, this example being for the South African Artillery; they were worn in pairs on either side of the sun helmet.

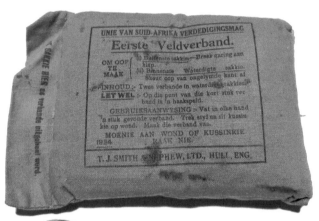

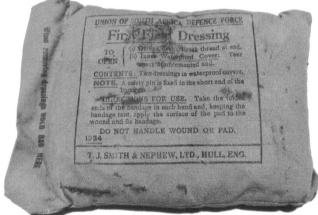

The Union of South Africa ordered first field dressings from companies such as Smith & Nephew in England during the interwar years. Each packet had bilingual instructions on it, with one side in English and the other in Afrikaans. This dressing dates from 1934 and was purchased as part of South Africa's expansion of its armed forces in the 1930s.

Field and shell dressings, along with other small items of medical equipment, were carried by a unit's stretcher-bearer in a shell dressing bag. Throughout most of the interwar period, the old First World War pattern remained in use, distinguished from later designs by the leather-edged canvas and leather closure straps to secure the top flap. Stretcher-bearers were essential in colonial warfare as the size of forces was often too small to warrant an attached Royal Army Medical Corps doctor and a stretcher-bearer could provide immediate assistance to a casualty.

PLAYER'S CIGARETTES

REGIMENT LOUW WEPENER

Regiment Louw Wepener was founded in 1934 as part of the Union of South Africa's expansion of its armed forces. The regiment was an Afrikaans-speaking unit of the Citizen Force and was based in Ladybrand, but recruited from across the Orange Free State. This sergeant of the newly formed regiment wears a grey-green uniform that was issued in place of khaki for service on the veldt. The jacket, shorts and puttees are made in this colour, the latter being secured with yellow cotton tapes. Likewise, his sun helmet is in the same colour fabric with the regimental badge affixed to the front and the yellow-over-black flash of the unit on his puggaree.

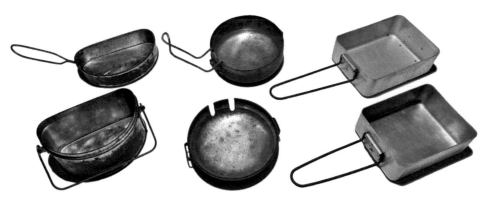

A number of different mess tins were used between the wars. The D-shaped mess tin (*left*) was standard issue to the infantry throughout the interwar period, the design dating back to the Napoleonic Wars. Cavalry and artillery were issued with circular tins (*centre*), secured with a leather strap. By the 1930s, the British Empire began a move to modernise their mess tins, introducing aluminium, which was more hygienic than tinned steel (*right*). All the different designs of mess tin opened into two pans. Traditionally, the shallower of the two was used for frying food, while the deep half could be used to boil liquids such as tea or stews.

The Union of South Africa was the first country in the Empire to issue aluminium mess tins on a large scale to its soldiers. They are clearly marked with the Broad Arrow within a 'U', indicating they were the property of the UDF, and this example was made by the London Aluminium Company Ltd in 1935.

The aluminium mess tins were issued with canvas bags to store them in when not in use. These were simple cotton bags with a drawstring closure. This example was made by Piggott Brothers & Co. Ltd and dates from 1938.

The D-shaped mess tin remained in service with much of the British Empire until the outbreak of the Second World War. It was often carried in a canvas pouch to reduce the danger from rattling and to prevent light being reflected off the metal surface. Many variations of the case existed; this example secures at the front with a single button and flap.

South African military forces did not fight an external enemy in the interwar period, but were used regularly in support of the civilian powers to put down rebellions and strikes. In February 1922, a strike by coal miners grew increasingly violent, with clashes between the strikers and the local police forces in the Witwatersrand region. By March, it was clear to the government in South Africa that the police had lost all control of the situation and it was agreed to send in the UDF to supress the rioting and restore order. The UDF Permanent Force was supported by 14,000 members of the Active Citizen Force and reservists were called back to active service. Martial law was declared in several parts of Witwatersrand and violent clashes erupted between the strikers and the military. The strikers held positions in Benoni, Springs, Boksburg, Brakpan and Johannesburg, which were bombed by the newly formed South African Air Force (SAAF). This act seemed to bring the strikers to the negotiating table and the strike ended on 17 March 1922. The UDF and local police lost forty-three men and the SAAF had two dead, two injured and two aircraft damaged beyond repair.

As well as seeing action against striking white miners, the UDF was also used to supress local black tribesmen, the region seeing a number of minor skirmishes over this period.

South Africa was given control of several German colonies in the aftermath of the First World War and inherited many of the local difficulties that the Germans had encountered. If the local tribesmen had hoped for a more sympathetic regime after the war, they were to be disappointed and it must be said that the paranoia of the white settlers in the region unduly influenced the South African administration. A series of incidents occurred with the Bondelswarts and the Rehoboth Basters tribes in the early interwar period. One of the most memorable skirmishes was in 1932, when the UDF was deployed against Chief Ipumbu of the Ukuambi Tribe. The chief had caused trouble in the 1920s by defying the authorities and launching raids against other tribes and then refusing to hand over the requisite number of cattle when issued fines for this behaviour. Added to this, he was actively trying to discourage Christian missionaries in his tribal region and in 1931 matters came to a head. Chief Ipumbu insisted that Christian girls in his tribe take part in the traditional puberty rights of the tribe and the girls fled to the safety of the Finnish Mission. In December 1931 he attempted to take his own daughter as his wife, against tribal tradition, and when the girl managed to escape her father she again fled to the mission. Ipumbu and 300 of his men, armed with rifles, marched on the mission and searched the buildings. Luckily, his daughter had already been smuggled out. This was the last straw for the authorities, who fined the chief ten head of cattle, which was rapidly increased to fifty as the chief ignored the demands. A final ultimatum came and went and in 1932 it was agreed to take military action with the opinion of the local political agent being that most of the tribe of 8,000 would welcome the overthrow of Ipumbu. Two Crossley armoured cars were sent to the chief's kraal, supported by aircraft. The morning of 15 August 1932 saw the deserted kraal bombed by the SAAF. After the air assault, men from the armoured cars were deployed to burn the kraal to the ground, but they were hindered by a large swarm of bees that had been angered by the bombing. The men used their Very flare pistols to fire smoke and keep the bees at bay while they set the fire. Fifty head of cattle had been killed by the bombing and given that this was the same as the fine imposed on Ipumbu, the matter was agreed to have been settled. With such a loss of face, the recalcitrant chief stepped down and went into exile, and peace was restored.

Anti-war feelings among the general public, limited funds, low priorities for defence and an increasing feeling of independence from the mother country made the interwar period an interesting time for all of the governments of the Empire and their militaries. In all cases, local forces were allowed to atrophy throughout the 1920s and early 1930s and it was only from around 1935 that investment started once more in the military. This ensured that when war broke out in 1939, the Empire was in a position to help Great Britain with at least some form of modern armed forces at their disposal. Without her allies across the Empire, it is highly unlikely that Great Britain would have survived the tumultuous early years of the Second World War until the US joined the fray. In that respect Britain was, by necessity, grateful to the dominion politicians and military leaders who started the urgent process of rearmament in the final years of peace.

Competition played an important part in army life between the wars. Along with sporting events, platoons and companies competed against each other in military contests such as marksmanship. Trophies were awarded to the team that achieved the highest score with particular weapons: here, rifles and the Lewis gun.

This Verner's pattern prismatic compass Mk VIII was manufactured in India in 1918. These compasses were highly accurate and sophisticated instruments for their era, allowing very precise calculations to be made. They were used as much for plotting indirect artillery and machine-gun fire as they were for map work. This prismatic compass includes a red rubber ring on the base that prevents it from sliding about on an unstable surface. A folding glass prism ensures accurate map readings and radium paint on the compass dial allowed it to glow in the dark. This example was manufactured by the Mathematical Instrument Office in Calcutta. This company was contracted to provide all the surveying equipment needed by the Indian Government and also provided binoculars and compasses to the Indian Army.

Selected Bibliography

Bates, Stuart, with Peter Suciu, *The Wolseley Helmet in Pictures from Omdurman to El Alamein* (PSB Publishing, 2009).

Brayley, Martin, and Richard Ingram, *Khaki Drill and Jungle Green: British Tropical Uniforms 1939–1945 in Colour Photographs* (Marlborough: Crowood Press, 2000).

Brayley, Martin, *Royal Navy Uniforms 1930–1945* (Marlborough: Crowood Press, 2014).

Landers, Rick, *'Saddle Up', Australian Load Carrying Equipment of British, American & Local Origin* (Rick Landers, 1998).

Mayer-Maguire, Thomas and Brian Baker, *British Military Respirators and Anti-Gas Equipment of the Two World Wars* (Marlborough: Crowood Press, 2015).

Summers, Jack, *Tangled Web: Canadian Infantry Accoutrements 1855–1985* (Canadian War Museum Historical Publications, 1991).

Tyler, Grant, *Drab Serge and Khaki Drill: The Foreign Service, Universal Service, Battle and Combat Dress Jackets of the Canadian Army 1899–2003* (Parks Canada, 2003).

www.karkeeweb.com